Advanced praise for *Yoga Mind*
by Suzan Colón

"Most books on yoga explain how to achieve peace through teaching about body postures. Although *Yoga Mind* includes physical techniques, this book does much more. Through her engaging, accessible style, Suzan Colón explains the principles and attitudes that lead to true inner transformation by sharing practices that anyone can do—no matter what age you are or what shape your body is in. I highly recommend this book."

—James Baraz, author of *Awakening Joy* and
cofounder of Spirit Rock Meditation Center, Woodacre, CA

"What a refreshing read! It is the yoga that we practice off the mat and in our hearts and minds that can truly transform ourselves and our world. Suzan Colón has written the yoga book that the world most needs right now."

—Jo Sgammato, *New York Times* bestselling author

"I'd read anything Suzan Colón writes—her words are always full of heart, soul, and smarts. Now she takes that talent to the topic of Yoga, organizing our way to centeredness, steadiness, easefulness, mindfulness, and balance from the inside out. Who couldn't use more of that every day?"

—Julie Morgenstern, *New York Times* bestselling
author of *Organizing from the Inside Out*
and the forthcoming *Time to Parent*

"*Yoga Mind* gets to the heart of yoga by exploring practical and accessible ways anyone can bring yoga into their life, even if they can't do a single pose. It's wonderful to have a resource that exposes these powerful tools and shows us how to implement them in order to bring more peace and ease into our everyday life."

—Jivana Heyman, founder of Accessible Yoga

"What a refreshing and empowering book. Suzan's embodiment of yoga through her book gives readers permission to make peace with ourselves and our bodies through this practice. Thank you for this inspiring read."

—Dianne Bondy, yoga educator and creator of the Yoga for All movement

"Suzan Colón is a wise, sensitive, and irresistibly sane guide who shares the true meaning and deeper gifts of yoga and friendship. Reading this beautiful offering of a book and working with the practices described here will change your life. A balm for anyone who is struggling to live better and more truly."

—Jessica Berger Gross, author of *Estranged* and *enLIGHTened*

"*Yoga Mind* takes us on a deep and delightful thirty day (and life-time) journey on how yoga can benefit our day-to-day lives. There is practical wisdom on each page, delivered with such wit that I found myself laughing out loud while reading on the subway. The format of the book is ingenious: It is a personal story of deal-ing with tragedy, mixed with specific day-by-day lesson plans for spiritual growth, and one of the most concise and clear summaries of the yogic path that you will find anywhere. You will savor this book for a long, long time."

—Swami Asokananda, President, Integral Yoga Institute of New York City

yoga mind

journey beyond the physical

*30 days to enhance your practice
and revolutionize your life
from the inside out*

Suzan Colón

SCRIBNER

New York   London   Toronto   Sydney   New Delhi

Scribner
An Imprint of Simon & Schuster, Inc.
1230 Avenue of the Americas
New York, NY 10020

First Scribner trade paperback edition February 2018

SCRIBNER and design are registered trademarks of The Gale Group, Inc., used under license by Simon & Schuster, Inc., the publisher of this work.

For information about special discounts for bulk purchases, please contact Simon & Schuster Special Sales at 1-866-506-1949 or business@simonandschuster.com.

The Simon & Schuster Speakers Bureau can bring authors to your live event. For more information or to book an event, contact the Simon & Schuster Speakers Bureau at 1-866-248-3049 or visit our website at www.simonspeakers.com.

Interior design by Jaime Putorti

Manufactured in the United States of America

10 9 8 7 6 5 4 3 2

Library of Congress Cataloging-in-Publication Data is available.

ISBN 978-1-5011-6886-4
ISBN 978-1-5011-6888-8 (ebook)

contents

To Mom, Dad, and Nathan, with all my heart.

And to you, dear reader, divine light.
May your life be peaceful, easeful, useful,
and filled with lasting happiness.

You can't stop the waves, but you can learn to surf.
—Sri Swami Satchidananda

yoga
mind

take a deep breath

O kay, you can come in now."

I looked up at Francesco's sister, her face pale and thin with worry, and I tried to set my own expression into something normal. I wasn't sure what, exactly, normal might be, under the circumstances.

A few weeks earlier, my friend Francesco Clark had taken a joyful dive into a pool and broken his neck. He'd gone from being an able-bodied person to being a quadriplegic in less than a breath. Somehow he'd survived the shattering of his vertebrae and nearly drowning, then being transported by medical helicopter to a trauma center—a lifesaving measure that also carried the risk of splintered bones severing more spinal nerves with even the slightest movement. As doctors raced Fran into surgery to stabilize his spine and relieve the pressure in his neck that was slowly suffocating him, they called his parents so he could say good-bye in case he didn't live through the seven-hour operation. His mother, on vacation with his father and sister in

Florida, told Fran he would be all right, hung up the phone, and collapsed.

But Francesco did survive the operation, and the trauma, both physical and emotional, that came with his accident. By surviving, he created a new plane of relativity: the blessings within a curse. Now, after weeks in the ICU, he was well enough to receive visitors other than a priest and next of kin.

I not only wanted to see him; after his near-death experiences I felt a desperate *need* to see my friend in the flesh, to see for myself that he was truly alive. But now it felt as though I couldn't move from the hospital waiting room chair. I knew he'd be changed; he would likely be in a wheelchair. But how else had this grave situation affected him? I was afraid of how different he'd be compared to the last time I'd seen him.

Francesco and I met in 2001 while working at *Mademoiselle* magazine, where he was the assistant to the entertainment editor, Geri Richter Campbell. I was an editor-at-large, writing cover stories on celebrities. Geri had hired Fran straight out of college and spent the days leading up to his start date bragging about her new model-handsome assistant who spoke three languages. After he began working with us, Geri and I both proudly announced that we had a new best friend/little brother. Fran was a combination of well-traveled worldliness and wide-eyed-kid excitement. He could be sophisticated one minute and goofy the next, witty and clever while entirely unjaded. Everyone at the magazine predicted that he'd be running a major empire before he was thirty and yet would remain a total sweetheart. When *Mademoiselle* folded a month after the September 11 terrorist attacks on the

World Trade Center, Geri, Fran, and I all pinky-swore that we'd stay in touch. Then, like everyone else, we got really busy.

Catch-up dates were planned and rescheduled endlessly. (This was before Facebook, where keeping in touch would've meant liking one another's posts.) Somehow a whole year went by. Then one afternoon I got a frantic call from Geri telling me Fran had nearly died. The details spilled out of her in a trembling ramble—he dove into a pool, it was dark, it was the shallow end, he couldn't see, he broke his neck, he's paralyzed—and I sank to the floor as I wept, thinking, *Why didn't I try harder to see him?*

I'd learned when I was a child that life could pull a devastating vanishing act. During one of their nightly calls, my nana told my mother she'd see us that coming weekend as usual, signed off with love, and quietly had an aneurysm. One minute there, the next minute gone. The lesson was buried in my marrow. As I grew up, my feelings toward people close to me careened between intense gratitude for having them and numb terror over losing them. I resolved that I would see Francesco as soon as the hospital would allow it.

Now that I was finally able to see him, I couldn't move, and the mild scent of hospital antiseptic was trapped in my held breath. What scared me was not imagining the physical changes Fran would have undergone after this catastrophic accident, but that *he*, his essence and core, might have been broken as well.

After a moment I got to my feet and followed Fran's sister, Charlotte, into his room. Their parents and grandmother stood in a huddle looking downward, which is what you do when a person is not on eye level because he's sitting in a wheelchair. As

Charlotte and I came into the room, the family turned toward us. Their faces were gray with the still-fresh shock of having nearly lost Francesco, ironically to a single carefree moment: at the start of a holiday weekend, with an exciting new job beginning the following week and the sense that the coming years would be as great as the previous twenty-four had been, Fran had taken a leap . . .

"*Heyyyy!*" Francesco gave me his usual huge grin, now incongruous in this fluorescent-lit hospital room so heavy with emotion. Normally he would've bounded over and given me one of his huge, happy-puppy hugs. But now he was motionless in the wheelchair, his arms and legs carefully arranged in resting positions. A thick brace encased his torso and held up his head, immobilizing his spine while his cracked vertebrae healed. His body was unnaturally still; my brain understood what had happened, but my visceral reaction was *No, this isn't right.* As I took all this in, I felt my own legs becoming unstable.

I wasn't sure what to do next. Was it okay to hug him? That thick body brace said no. I took his hand and felt my stomach go cold when I realized he couldn't feel my fingers grasping his. *What do I do?* Glowing coals of nervousness flared brighter, and the first thing that came into my mind fell out of my mouth.

"Stupid question," I said, "but how are you?"

"Actually, I'm great," Fran said immediately, and oh thank God, his usual optimism was intact. "Did you know I nearly died? I'm really lucky to be here."

His surprising perspective gave the moment the quality of an exhalation of relief. The feeling was not unlike bracing for more turbulence in a plane and then finding the rough clouds have passed to allow for smooth travel. Either to avoid further awkwardness or because he didn't want to talk about his accident, Fran said, "How are *you* doing? Wait, didn't I hear you just graduated from a yoga teacher training course?"

Now I did have to sit down, not only to bring myself to eye level with Fran, but because a thought that had been lurking in the back of my mind suddenly attacked me. Yes, I had just graduated from yoga teacher training. For the past four months, I'd been immersed in all aspects of yoga—how to teach asana (the physical poses) and learning about yoga's philosophy and spirituality. I could now instruct classrooms full of beginner-level students in poses ranging from simple cross-legged sitting positions to challenging twists, balances, and even shoulder stands. I'd taken this training so I could help people feel as good as I did when I practiced yoga. Now a friend whose place in my heart was impervious to time and distance needed help. But Francesco couldn't move anything except his face, to smile with hope. How could I, a newly minted yoga teacher, possibly help him?

The spiritual tools of yoga provided the answer.

* * *

Like most people, I thought yoga was a form of exercise—those twisty, bendy, gymnastic postures performed by young, lithe women (and the occasional man). About a decade before the accident that left Francesco unable to move, I'd started looking into yoga because I really needed to move. As a longtime writer for magazines including *O, The Oprah Magazine*; *Harper's*

Bazaar; and *Good Housekeeping*, as well as the author of several books, I spent most of my days sitting at a desk. We've recently heard a great deal about the unhealthy effects of sitting for long periods of time, but back then, I was my own case study: everything hurt. I knew I needed exercise, as well as some form of stress reduction that would help me deal with the pressures of work and life in general. Yoga, I'd heard, offered both.

Integral Yoga Institute wasn't far from where I lived, and I'd passed by the peach-colored building in New York City's West Village hundreds of times over the years. One day I walked in, and just entering the reception area felt like taking a deep, relaxing breath. The people working there and the students checking in for classes all seemed so *calm*. Soothing pastel hues began on the walls of the bookstore; led upstairs to studios named Lavender, Aqua, Gold, Lotus, and Heaven; and continued throughout a building that was not just a yoga studio but an ashram, a place where people lived while they studied yoga.

The quiet, mellow environment helped relax muscles I didn't realize were tense, even before the yoga class began. Once the teacher began leading us through a breathing exercise, during which I took fuller, more substantive breaths than I could recall taking in some time, I had an unexpected reaction: I began to weep with relief. I hadn't realized how much stuff—stress, emotions, thoughts of the past, worries about the future—I'd been holding in, until yoga showed me how to safely release it.

The far more common reaction to being in an Integral Yoga class is a happy sigh and a soft smile. Shoulders loosen away from ears, eyes previously laser-focused on phones drift closed, and you can feel the students' stress melting away. And that's before they've done a single pose.

As a student at Integral Yoga, then as a teacher and eventually a teacher trainer, I've learned that yoga is much, much more than just the poses, or asana. This ancient Eastern practice has its own philosophy, ethical principles, and tools that form a design for living.

Yet here in the West, the primary focus is on yoga's physical practice. That was my primary focus, too; it's through the door of asana that most people discover yoga's bigger picture. It wasn't until Francesco's accident that I began to truly understand that yoga is a wide and welcoming spiritual path, one that anybody, regardless of age, religion, or physical ability, can walk—even if they can't walk at all.

In order to understand the tools of yoga and begin to see how useful they can be, it helps to have some background information. Yoga, like Buddhism, is not a religion. It can be compared in a general sense to philosophy or spirituality in that people of any religion can, and do, make use of yoga's secular tools. Both yoga and Buddhism were born thousands of years ago in India, where the Sanskrit word *yoga* means "union"— union with something greater than ourselves, union of body and mind through breathing, union that comes when we release the false idea of aloneness that creates harmful feelings and habits and come to understand that we are all connected. Yogic sages, people who were dedicated to helping others attain a higher level of living, created a combination of breathing practices, accessible approaches to meditation, philosophy and ethics, physical exercise, and spiritual tools to navigate life with courage, serenity, joy, good health, compassion, and grace.

Today, an estimated thirty-six million people in America engage in some form of yoga. Because it is so effective at reducing stress, it is constantly being adapted for different populations and different needs. Yoga has gone from studios to corporate boardrooms, schools, hospitals, rehabilitation centers, and more. The CEOs and employees of Fortune 500 companies do it, as do children in high-crime areas, veterans returning from wars, seniors in elder-care centers . . . And the list of those who are experiencing the stress-relieving, health-giving benefits of yoga is growing all the time.

Yet this is still not all that yoga is, or can be. Yoga goes well beyond a form of physical exercise; it's a spiritual toolkit we can use in all areas of our lives, every day—and not just for the hour or so we're on the mat. You can think of yoga as an ancient spiritual technology for wellness and well-being. It has survived for thousands of years and has become more widespread and popular in our modern times for one reason: it works. Its tools are not only relevant today, they're more necessary than ever in our constantly changing, stress-filled times. And you don't have to do the physical asana practice in order to gain incredible benefit from using yoga's tools. My friend Francesco, who couldn't move at all, was one of the best yoga students I ever had.

He was also one of the greatest yoga teachers I will ever have. Through Francesco, the tools of yoga and their potential for subtle but powerful life shifts came vividly alive, and I came to understand that yoga isn't something you do. It's something you live, practicing each day, so that you can become the best version of yourself.

This was the vision of Swami Satchidananda, the founder of Integral Yoga, where I studied and became a yoga teacher. Born in India in 1914, Swami Satchidananda (whose name translates from Sanskrit as "truth, knowledge, bliss") was asked by artist Peter Max and filmmaker Conrad Rooks to come to America in the late 1960s, a time of deep social turmoil—protests, rioting, racism, rampant drug use. It doesn't sound all that different from today.

The swami spoke about yoga's tools to people hungry for positive change, for themselves and for the world. Swami Satchidananda's message of peace had such a profound impact on people that he was brought by helicopter to the Woodstock music festival to give an opening address that would calm the swelling crowds. The event, attended by over four hundred thousand, continued peacefully over four days.

The swami, affectionately called Gurudev ("beloved teacher"), made world peace his life's work, and his message of "Easeful body, peaceful mind, useful life" had wide-ranging influence. He met with Pope Paul VI, the Dalai Lama, President George H. W. Bush, and President Bill Clinton. He was a guest speaker at the international religious assembly for the United Nations Special Session on Disarmament. His whole-life teachings of yoga influenced the groundbreaking heart-disease-reversal work of Dean Ornish, MD; the Commonweal Cancer Help Program formulated by Michael Lerner, MD; and other current whole-being health care systems. Dr. Wayne Dyer said of Swami Satchidananda, "He helped me to raise my consciousness

to a place of being more peaceful, more loving." Swami Satchidananda's interpretation of yoga, designed to be as accessible as
possible to all who need it, has touched the lives of countless
people, including me and Francesco. And now, you.

✳

We know why we should practice physical yoga—to have a healthy,
flexible body. But why do we need a flexible Yoga Mind? Why has
yoga been a predominantly spiritual practice for thousands of years,
and why is it so necessary for our lives right now?

Yoga gives us the opportunity to live our lives more fully,
deeply, authentically, and organically. Its spiritual tools teach
us to recognize and get past obstacles that hold us back. They
make broad concepts like mindfulness and meditation simpler,
able to fit into our busy days and lives. They help us deal with
long-standing issues that cause suffering, and enhance the present moment. They help us make subtle shifts that lead to lasting
change. And because, simply put, sometimes everything is not
going to be okay.

Life challenges happen to everyone. There are a multitude of
different types—illness, job loss, divorce, you name it. In these
situations, it's just not "all good," and if some well-meaning person says, "Everything happens for a reason," our reaction is less
soothed and maybe even more upset, wondering what kind of
world we live in if that could be true.

At the time I found Integral Yoga, I was not aware that I
was reaching for an ideal of life where everything was perfect—
when, someday, I'd have the perfect job, the perfect home, the

perfect relationship, the perfect body, and on and on. Yoga, and particularly Integral Yoga, offered something far more realistic and attainable: balance.

This ashram full of vibrant people of all kinds, including those with injuries, illnesses, frailties that come with age, and varying abilities, even a teacher in a wheelchair and a vision-impaired student (Integral was the only yoga studio that would allow her service dog in the building), was an example of real life. Things happen, and we can work with them. Swami Satchidananda knew that yoga could help us achieve balance. "You can't stop the waves," he said, "but you can learn how to surf." After I heard that, I was finally able to release unattainable ideals of perfection and begin to truly live my life.

Yoga's spiritual tools address the waves of life, from the smooth, happy times to those very not-okay times when we fall ill, when someone we love leaves or dies, when our lives turn inside out and our most vulnerable parts are exposed. Developing a Yoga Mind can help us find our own natural reserves of strength and resilience, and make them stronger. It does the same for the best parts of ourselves, showing us how to cultivate the habits and traits we aspire to embody. The spiritual practice of yoga helps us to shine brightly by helping us see the divine light already within us. With a yoga body, you can do impressive poses; with a Yoga Mind, you can do anything.

✳

I learned this over twenty-five years of practicing yoga and working with individual clients, classes of students and groups of teacher trainees, executives in corporate boardrooms, educators in seminars, and hospital staff, and by working with Francesco every week for over a year after his accident. The program in this book is an interpretation of the yoga tools used on my own spiritual path, Francesco's, and that of others (whom I've written as composite characters to respect their privacy).

I've been fortunate enough to learn from monks living in yoga ashrams, but I'm an average woman living in the everyday world. Therefore, my interpretations of these ancient concepts may be somewhat nontraditional. But I know that using these tools to develop a Yoga Mind works because they've gotten me through challenging situations and taught me how to live a happier life.

There are many tools in yoga, but I've chosen the ones that I've found most adaptable to our daily lives, and most helpful for achieving the goals of living authentically and fully; being more mindful; getting through the things that can fragment us with grace; finding a sense of purpose and meaning in our lives; and being happier.

These thirty yoga tools are organized into sections based on how they complement one another. The order they're in is modeled after the gentle, gradual process of an Integral Yoga class, starting with learning how to breathe your way to a more relaxed, receptive state of being in which you can do interior spiritual work. (Don't worry, it's much easier than it sounds!) Each day, a new yoga tool will be introduced. You'll learn how to apply it through a real-life experience, and then you'll find an exercise so you can try the tool out. These exercises are simple and won't take much time, but their effects are palpable.

In Integral Yoga classes, there are brief periods of rest in a relaxed pose called Savasana. Between each group of yoga tools and their exercises, you will find a Savasana, a pause with a short overview of the upcoming tools and the kind of work that you will be doing:

Part 1: Grounding and Centering, where we begin with simple practices that give you the foundation of the Yoga Mind program.

Part 2: Mindful Shifts, where the seeds of positive change are subtle but noticeable.

Part 3: Finding Your Balance, where you maintain equilibrium while seeing and feeling the effects of the work you're doing.

Part 4: Steadiness and Easefulness, where you add to your established practice with tools to take it out into the world.

The point of yoga is to be and feel your best not just for an hour on the mat when you can get to class, but throughout your day, throughout your life. We just need a guide, some practical examples, and the occasional reminder. This book was designed to travel with you, to be there on your desk at work or in your bag. Think of it as your constant companion on your spiritual path.

After you work the program in order, you can use the yoga tools again in a variety of ways. Choose tools at random each day. Pick a tool and make it your focus for a week. When you have a particular need, meditate on a mantra; you'll find a number of these affirmations throughout the program. The yoga tools are also listed by category in the appendix, so if you need a certain type of tool, you'll have a quick reference guide.

For this kind of yoga, you don't need any fancy clothing, a mat, or big chunks of time. You don't need to be physically fit or particularly flexible, other than having an open mind. All you need are a simple notebook to keep track of feelings and changes along the way, and a desire to create positive shifts in your life. You don't have to wait for those shifts to maybe, hopefully happen someday. The yoga tools show you how to create them.

When I found yoga, the asana practice felt like a physical form of prayer. My only problem was how to take that prayer beyond the mat. I found the answer by using the yoga tools to help me develop a Yoga Mind. They taught me how to live life fully, see meaning and value in experiences of all kinds, and find sweet richness in simple moments. They gave me strength and resilience. They can do this for you, too.

The desire to help is something every being has within, to the point that it's more of an instinct than a choice. Initially I didn't know how I could help Francesco. But it is in absolute darkness that stars shine most brightly. It is from tremendous pressure that diamonds are formed. And so it was that in a very challenging time for him, and for me, the true gifts of yoga were revealed. It is a great gift to be able to share them with you now.

Namaste, the traditional yoga greeting, means, "I see the divine light in you." May this book help you see the divine light that burns so brightly within you.

grounding and centering

At the start of each Integral Yoga class, there is a period of grounding and centering—a space of time and guidance that allows students to become settled and prepare for the class. They've just come rushing in, all stressed out from a day of work and the mad dash to get to class. They're breathless and still thinking about things they didn't get to or what they'll be doing later, their minds jumping from the past to the future.

For this reason, we pause . . . take a few full, relaxing breaths . . . and just sit. Let the mind and the body become calm. Come into the present moment. And gently orient ourselves toward what is ahead. Everything in a yoga class is beneficial, but the benefits grow when students hear what they'll be doing and how the exercises work. So, in this and other Savasana sections to come, we'll briefly go over the upcoming yoga tools and what you'll gain from them.

This first group of yoga tools is the equivalent of starting a yoga class with gentle stretching exercises that would warm you up for more challenging poses. Some of the practices will be used throughout the program. In this section, you will learn about:

✳ **Sankalpa**—An intention, more powerful than a resolution or a promise, that you'll set and that will carry you throughout the course.

✳ **Deergha Swasam**—A breathing exercise that you'll do to begin each day feeling calm and balanced, and that you can do whenever you feel stress.

✳ **Ahimsa**—Yoga's principle of non-harming, ahimsa teaches us how to be free of self-sabotaging thoughts and actions.

✳ **Mantra**—A powerful affirmation that protects your mind against the painful effects of negative thinking.

✳ **Dharana**—The first step toward meditation, this tool helps you strengthen your ability to concentrate.

✳ **Sangha**—A spiritual community of people like yourself who provide support and keep each other going on the path toward their goals.

✳ **Brahmacharya**—A way of harnessing your energy to maximize your effectiveness and accomplish what's important to you.

* **Asana**—The physical part of your program, this section is about finding movement that works for you, even if it's visualization meditation, which has surprising effects.

Don't worry about the pronunciations of the Sanskrit words; you'll find that these tools are familiar concepts with different names. Their basis in yoga will show you new ways they can be viewed, and the stories that illustrate them will give you examples of how they can be applied in your own life. At the end of each chapter, there is an exercise for you to do that day. It won't be complex, but these simple practices bring about substantial shifts and ease you into the rhythm of this program.

Feeling centered and ready? Let's take a deep, relaxing breath and begin.

day 1

sankalpa

(san-KAL-pa)
Setting an intention;
making a spiritual resolution.

Each January, I made the list: *Lose five pounds. No, make it ten. Well, start with five and see how you do. Go to the gym. Take up running (maybe when the weather gets warmer). Get the book on that new diet* [which, depending on the year and fad, would be low calorie, low fat, low carb, vegetarian, vegan, Paleo, etc.]. And by the first week of March, the list would be sticking out of the first quarter of the mostly unread diet book, right next to my unused sneakers. My intentions were good, but my New Year's resolutions never stuck.

Sankalpas, on the other hand, never failed.

Wheelchair be damned, with each visit to the hospital over the next two weeks, Francesco and I slipped right back into the routine we'd had at work: We gossiped. We talked about who had gotten a new job, who had broken up with whom, and other news about former colleagues and celebrities. None of it was mean-spirited, and I knew my yoga teachers would have given me a pass on the not-very-spiritual activity of gossiping if they'd seen the relief on Francesco's grandmother's face when she heard him laughing. Nonni—a variation of the Italian word *nonna*, or "grandmother"—spoke only Italian and didn't understand what we were talking about, but her grandson's laughter—music that cut through the crisis—was universal.

On my long walks home from the hospital, though, I wept. The shocking near loss of a friend, and one so young, had abated and was replaced by a new sadness: helpless frustration. I'd become a yoga teacher so I could help people. I'd been especially drawn toward helping people who thought yoga wasn't accessible to them—seniors, or "elders," as they were respectfully called at Integral Yoga, as well as people with arthritis and other debilitating conditions and illnesses. I wanted to show them that anyone could do yoga.

Would that turn out to mean anyone *but* Fran, and all the other people in his ward who were waking up each day to the new reality of limbs that didn't move anymore and machines that breathed for them? That wasn't something I could accept. Some things had to be acknowledged; it was a fact that Francesco was gravely injured. He had an incomplete spinal cord injury, meaning that his spinal cord had not been completely severed. To the degree that his had, though, doctors felt it was unlikely he would use his hands, arms, or legs again. Things we take for granted, like getting up to go to the bathroom or picking up a cup of coffee for a sip, were now for Francesco in the same league as climbing Mount Everest.

But the idea that yoga couldn't help him was something I wouldn't even consider. I was a true believer in the power of yoga to help injuries of all types, physical, emotional, or spiritual—not cure, necessarily, but improve the lives of the people working with them. I'd personally seen amazing things during my years of practicing at Integral Yoga, a place that attracted not just the young and healthy but elders who took the elevator because their arthritic knees wouldn't let them climb the stairs. As part of my teacher training, I'd taken a Gentle Yoga class that included a ninety-year-old woman whose aide brought her into the room in a wheelchair. The aide eased her onto a setup of bolsters and blankets that the teacher had prepared on a yoga mat. There, this beautiful elder lifted her arm—the only part of her body she was able to move—gracefully in time with the rest of the students doing modified poses. The smile she wore throughout the class dissolved any doubt that might have remained in me and released it through tears of wonder. That woman, that beautiful elder who could barely move, was doing yoga.

And so, I resolved, could Fran. There was a way; there had to be. I just couldn't see it yet. I had faith that it would be revealed. In the meantime, I did what I could: I set a sankalpa.

Yoga's version of a resolution, a sankalpa is different from the promises we make to ourselves each January 1. It's less of a rigid, ironclad mandate and more of an intention. What makes a sankalpa more effective than a resolution is that it's usually directed toward someone other than ourselves.

At the start of many Integral Yoga classes, the teacher would instruct students to place the palms of their hands together at their hearts in what looked like a prayer. "Now, if you like, you can set a sankalpa, an intention," the teacher would offer. "You can dedicate your practice today to someone in need. Or, if you need extra help with something, set your sankalpa toward that." I was intrigued by this word that seemed equal parts promise, resolution, and intention, yet more powerful than any of them.

Further resonant understanding came via teachings from Swami Satchidananda, the founder of Integral Yoga. "Don't have the word *impossible* in your vocabulary," he told his students. "Stand up and make an affirmation." He described a sankalpa as a strong decision and a pure thought based on the welfare of others. "Then," he said, "your sankalpa will be firm."

An estimated 40 percent of Americans make New Year's resolutions, but research from the University of Scranton suggests that the percentage of people who achieve what they set out to do is a measly (though victorious) 8 percent. The reasons vary as to why. The goals may be too large, like total life makeovers, or too vague, like "getting in shape" versus something specific, like training to run or walk a 5K.

Swami Satchidananda's words presented another possible explanation. My resolutions had always focused on me—losing weight, finding a boyfriend, getting a better-paying job, writing a book. There was nothing wrong with any of these goals, but because they were all about me, it was almost as easy to break them as to make them when the work of doing them got too hard. I hadn't tried making a resolution for someone else's benefit before. And I couldn't imagine, say, giving up on Francesco.

After my long, thoughtful walk home from the hospital, I arrived at the building where I lived, in a Manhattan neighborhood near Gramercy Park but not as chichi, and close to the East Village but not as cool. When I got inside my front door, I reflexively took off my shoes, a habit learned at the ashram. I fed Ethel, my black and white kitty, and almost without thought I went straight to my yoga mat and sat down. I lit a candle on a little altar I'd made from a box covered with a pretty shawl. I sat and let my awareness rest on my breathing for a few minutes. I didn't know exactly how this was supposed to go—some yoga ceremonies could be pretty elaborate, with special garments and chants—but when I'd made a sankalpa in class, it had been as simple as making a wish on a birthday.

I'm going to help Francesco, I thought as I brought my hands together in Anjali Mudra, the prayer position. Then I added, *Help me to help him. Show me the way.*

The following week, the answer came.

yoga mind practice:
Setting Your Sankalpa

In yoga, a sankalpa is a strong intention, usually in service of someone else. That doesn't mean you can't set a sankalpa for yourself, because more often than not, what benefits you will have a positive effect on others. You might set an intention to quit smoking or start exercising three times a week for the benefit of someone you love and who loves you; your being healthier will make them happier. You could set a sankalpa to manage your work hours differently so you can spend more time with your children, for them as well as for you. Now you've probably figured out the true power behind the sankalpa, what makes it so effective and gives it fuel to last: love. We may give up easily on promises made to ourselves, but we're far more likely to keep a promise that will help someone or something we care about deeply.

When teaching yoga asanas, the physical postures, an instructor will make adjustments with the gentlest touch possible. Here, as well, an attitude of gentleness will bring about the most positive, least painful changes. For example, hard-core workout regimens are often quickly abandoned because they're just too brutal. But you're more likely to stick with a form of fitness you enjoy, even if it takes longer to show results, because you look forward to it.

With this gentle attitude in mind, close your eyes and let your awareness rest on your breathing for a few moments. Allow yourself to consider parts of your life where you'd like to cultivate positive change, and then the good these changes might bring to others. If you'd like to start a fitness program, think of the joy your family would feel about your being healthier and living longer. If you'd like to get a new job, think of the benefit your skills could bring to a company that needs them. When your intentions are for the good of others, you can easily see how what is helpful to you would be helpful to them. It's a win-win.

Now imagine those benefits rippling outward. One of my students, K, began her goal of losing weight and getting fit so she could set a good example for her daughter. They began working out together, and soon K's husband wanted to join in, too. The whole family got fit and healthier, all because of K's intention to give her daughter a positive influence. Your actions have a ripple effect—sometimes seen, sometimes not, yet all important.

Now compose your sankalpa, using positive, encouraging language, and set it by writing it down on the first page of your Yoga Mind journal. If you wish, you can turn this practice into a puja, or spiritual ceremony, by lighting a candle, placing flowers on the table where you write, and adding a photo of the person for whom you're creating this sankalpa.

Your written sankalpa can be as short as a single sentence or as long as a paragraph. You don't need to go into great detail. The divine light within your heart knows the truth of your intention.

deergha swasam

(DEER-ga SWA-sam)
Deep three-part
breathing practice.

Take a deep breath.

How often do you say that to yourself, or find others suggesting it to you? I had to remind myself to take deep, calming breaths all the time when I worked at demanding office jobs. Most of my career was spent as a writer and editor at various magazines, though some of the editors in chief who ran them seemed to think that we were doing life-or-death triage in emergency rooms.

"This fashion layout is late!" an editor exclaimed during a staff meeting one day. "We've got to get this done on time! Today!"

I used to go along with this *every second counts!* TV-drama attitude and sometimes even enjoyed it; a sense of urgency makes people feel important. At lunch together, Francesco, Geri, and I would mock-complain about how busy we were. We felt even more puffed up when we were so busy that we couldn't take lunch at all, beavering away at our desks instead.

Francesco's accident was a massive perspective check. Now I knew someone who had been in a real life-or-death situation. It was hard to participate in the frantic urgency generated by typical work deadlines after that.

"Are you going to have that fashion copy done today?" the editor demanded.

Take a deep breath, I reminded myself. "I'll have it done this afternoon." I gave the description of those ruffled leggings and camouflage tops my full attention so I could leave work on time and visit Francesco.

The subway ride from the office to the hospital was becoming a familiar path. In the few weeks since Francesco had been moved from the ICU, I'd been a regular visitor. I never really questioned why I felt compelled to see him as often as I could. It was as though I had my own sense of urgency, though nothing was particularly critical now; Francesco was stable, his life no longer in danger. Yet I went to see him frequently, partly to cheer him up and also because of that strong feeling that there must be something more I could do to help him.

On the few days a week I didn't visit him at the hospital, I made sure to replenish myself with the meditative classes at Integral Yoga. Each time I went, my hand would touch the front door right next to an inscription that is part motto, part mission statement, part mantra. This legend was the goal of Integral

Yoga, and of all who taught there, as stated by Swami Satchidananda:

Easeful body, peaceful mind, useful life.

For me, the easeful body had come with asana, the physical practice of yoga. I felt healthy and moved with good flexibility for someone staring down her fortieth birthday at the time. Peaceful mind—well, sometimes. With editors implying that descriptions of ruffled leggings were a matter of national importance, trying to have a peaceful mind was another form of work.

The "useful life" part of the legend asked me to weigh the cumulative contents of my days. I believed then, and believe now, that each of us is important, making our own unique contributions to the world, and that the smallest gesture from one can change the life of another. But at the time, I was interviewing celebrities about romantic comedies and writing about fleeting fashion trends. One of my colleagues summed up the results of our labor by (partly) joking, "We work very hard to create bird-cage liners."

Sure, writing was a form of service, even the kind of light writing I was doing. I realized this in the months following the September 11 terrorist attacks on the World Trade Center. I told a friend that I was having trouble writing about silly things like actors and lipstick after such a devastating event. My friend said, "Are you kidding? Stories about movie stars and makeup are the only things keeping me sane these days." I felt good about that, but I wanted to do more. One of the reasons I'd taken yoga teacher training was to make a greater contribution of service in my life. I'd been helped by yoga; maybe I could help people by teaching yoga.

Francesco needed help more than anyone I knew. The quiet but strong sense that there must be something yoga could do for him accompanied me everywhere, faithful as a shadow on a sunny day.

"*Heyyyyy!*" Francesco's greeting to me was always the same, as was the huge grin that defied the grayness of his hospital room. I'd see this smile and think things might not be so bleak, though the research I'd done on spinal cord injuries of his extent never varied: Spinal cord nerves do not regenerate. What had been severed was gone. Regaining movement was highly unlikely.

Still, this was just weeks after his injury. Hope and a refusal to give in to fear were locked in a tight embrace.

Francesco's grandmother, Nonni, gave me what I guessed was a warm greeting in Italian. Fran murmured something to her, and she shrugged as more punctuated, musical syllables cascaded from her. "I reminded Nonni that you don't speak Italian," Fran told me. "She said that doesn't matter."

Nonni was part of a highly organized and efficient team of family members staying with Francesco at the hospital. Depending on the time of day, you'd find his father, Harold, a cardiologist; his mother, Mariella, who assisted in Dr. Clark's medical practice; his older brother, Michael, an IT specialist; his younger sister, Charlotte, a medical student; or Nonni watching over him. They oversaw every aspect of his treatment, and they kept him from falling into a pit of despondency when doctors said things like "He'll never move anything below his shoulders again" right in front of him.

"What?!" I felt my eyes bug out of my head when Fran told me this. "Why would the doctor say such a thing to you?"

"Medical staff are trained to be realistic and tell you only what they know," Fran explained. "But they don't leave a lot of room for what they *don't* know. I mean, when I first came in, they told me I was going to be on a ventilator for the rest of my life." His smile was sly. "And I said, 'Oh no I ain't.'"

"And I bet you've been reminding them of that ever since, frequently and loudly," I teased.

He laughed. "I've been talking so much I bet they *want* to put that ventilator tube back down my throat, just to shut me up."

This was as much as Fran wanted to talk about his situation. He asked me about work, and, knowing how he loved a good story, I turned the tale of the DEFCON 3–level fashion copy into a performance that almost included interpretive dance.

After a while of retelling similarly silly stories from our past, the present muscled back in. "Francesco, we have to take you for a few tests," a nurse said. Fran said he'd be back in a while as the nurse wheeled his chair out of the room.

Nonni smiled at me and patted the seat next to her for me to come over. Her face released the optimistic expression she'd been holding for her grandson. Now, though she knew I couldn't understand her, she began talking. Through my vague recollections of classes in French, a linguistic cousin of Italian, and Nonni's own interpretive pantomime, I was able to understand that she was telling me Francesco woke up every night crying from nightmares. As she spoke, she touched her legs and then whisked her hand away; he was dreaming that his legs were gone, or had been cut off.

Seeing his big smile and laughing with him over funny work stories made me want to believe that Fran was all right, but now I realized that of course he would be suffering, possibly even experiencing post-traumatic stress disorder. I'd usually heard the term associated with war veterans, but in yoga teacher training we'd learned that anyone who experiences a traumatic event can suffer from the effects of PTSD, including severe anxiety, nightmares, and panic attacks, even years after the inciting event.

Thinking of Francesco in this state made my urgent desire to help him even stronger, yet I continued to feel helpless as I sat in his hospital room during another visit, watching his sister spoon-feed him applesauce. If only I could figure out what could help Francesco—if not to get him walking again, at least to help with his stress.

During my yoga teacher training I'd read a lot of studies about yoga's ability to help people become calmer, and I knew it was true because of my own experience. If I had a stressful day at work, I'd go to a class, do some asana practice, and feel more relaxed. But this was not going to help Fran. There was no chance he'd be doing even a modified asana practice any time soon, or going back to running, previously his favorite form of exercise.

In one of my training classes, the teachers asked what we thought made yoga different from running or aerobics or any other type of physical fitness. We had many answers: yoga's slow, meditative pace; the spiritual foundation; the lack of thudding techno music. Our teachers shook their heads and said that power yoga and Vinyasa flow went at a fast pace, there was plenty of gym yoga without spirituality, and there were classes with all kinds of music. So what made yoga different from exercise?

The answers were mindfulness and breathing. Our teachers explained that in yoga's asana practice, awareness was not directed toward counting miles, speed, or repetitions; it was directed within, usually on the breath. And although you're obviously breathing in other forms of exercise, in yoga the breath is controlled at times through a practice called pranayama.

Prana is the Sanskrit word for what would translate to English as "life energy." It's the vitality you feel when you're at your best. It's also the kind of zing you'd get from a fresh orange at its peak, and the electricity that lights up a bulb. Prana is natural energy in all forms. In yogic theory, prana is taken into our bodies through sunlight, food, and air. *Ayama* means "to lengthen or extend." *Pranayama* means "cultivating greater, more lasting energy through breathing practices."

In yoga, there are many types of pranayama—breathing techniques designed to wake you up, cool you down, prepare you for meditation, and more. The foundation of all the pranayama practices is Deergha Swasam, or Deep Three-Part Breathing. This practice uses different parts of your torso to deepen your inhalations and exhalations.

As adults, most of our breathing takes place in the upper chest, a process known as thoracic breathing. It's not very efficient, being quite shallow—it uses only the tops of the lungs, which are small—and it mimics the breathing we do when the sympathetic nervous system responds to stress.

During a stressful event, the body prepares itself to fight or run away from perceived danger by ramping up respiration, releasing cortisol to get the heart pumping and insulin for a burst of energy, and shutting down digestion and other bodily functions. Though your mind can discern the differences between physical and emotional danger, your body can't, and it will have the same response to a rough day at the office as it would to a fire in your home.

If a person experiences stress on a consistent basis, this can lead to diabetes and heart disease from constantly elevated levels of insulin and cortisol, in addition to exhaustion, depression, and other side effects of prolonged stress response activity. By contrast, the parasympathetic nervous system generates the body's "rest and digest" state, or Peace Response, signaling to the body and brain that you're out of danger. The Peace Response can be induced through pranayama and meditation.

Also important is the spiritual aspect of the breath. My teachers often said, "The bridge between the body and the mind is the breath." This thinking is not limited to yoga; major religions, spiritual paths, and philosophies alike hold the breath sacred. The root of the word *inspiration* is the Latin *inspirare*, "to breathe into," though its meaning is more figurative than literal, as in being breathed into life by a divine spirit. Anyone seeing a newborn take that first breath would agree.

I watched Charlotte spoon-feeding Fran as if he were a baby and remembered my teachers telling us that we all start out breathing deeply, our little round baby bellies doing all the work. This is abdominal breathing, and Western medicine has found that it helps with respiratory ailments such as asthma and COPD by bringing more oxygen into your body. Abdominal breathing also reduces stress; it's the kind of breathing associated with the parasympathetic nervous system and the Peace Response.

I knew this firsthand, since *Take a deep breath* was my mantra at work. *The Deergha Swasam breathing practice could really help Fran*, I thought to myself, *if only—*

Whoa.

Even though Francesco's chest and belly were covered with a hospital gown and a blanket, I could see that they were rising and falling in a natural breathing rhythm. He'd been off the ventilator for weeks and was breathing on his own. If he was breathing on his own, he'd be able to do Deergha Swasam.

Francesco could do yoga.

"What?" he asked when he saw me smiling.

"Fran," I said cautiously, "would you like to try doing some yoga?"

His eyes lit up. "Charlotte," he said to his sister, "shut the door! I don't want the nurses coming in here and interrupting us." He looked back at me. "What are we going to do? How do I do this?"

"It's easy." I pulled my chair closer to his hospital bed. "You're already doing it."

yoga mind practice:
Deergha Swasam, Deep Three-Part Breathing

This is yoga's version of abdominal breathing, which is called three-part breath because it uses the three sections of your body's trunk—the abdomen, the lower ribs, and the upper chest—for each inhalation and exhalation. The breaths should feel full but not uncomfortable; you're not inhaling to the point of bursting or exhaling to the point of gasping. (If for some reason you do become a little light-headed, just return to normal breathing.) You're just taking fuller breaths than you might normally, in the same way as when you give a deep sigh of relaxation or relief.

There are two ways to approach Deergha Swasam. The first is by sitting up tall in a chair.

1. Place one hand on your belly and another on your chest, which will help you feel the motion of the breath. Exhale.

2. Inhale by gently expanding your abdomen and bring your breath to your lower ribs, then all the way to your upper chest. Exhale from your upper chest, relax your lower ribs, and gently pull in your abdomen.

3. Repeat for a few breaths, feeling the sensation of using different parts of your trunk to expand your breathing.

The second way is by lying down. This is especially helpful if you find that your belly goes out, instead of in, as you exhale. This is called reverse breathing, and it's a simple matter to correct: Lie down and place a book on your belly. Try to make the book rise as you inhale and fall as you exhale. Practice this a few times and then put the book aside. Place one hand on your belly and the other on your chest and follow the directions on page 38.

This pranayama practice is simple and subtle, but it is a powerful agent of change, because Deergha Swasam can reduce stress. Science can explain the physical effects of reducing stress and why it's so beneficial, but through personal experience, you'll discover what else can happen when you become calmer. Your intuition may become enhanced. Your ability to focus can improve. You may find that you're less reactive, more resilient. The effects of inducing calmness in the body and mind, and to what degree it is induced, vary from person to person. It will be interesting for you to note the differences in how you feel over the coming days and weeks in your Yoga Mind journal.

Because Three-Part Breathing can be so beneficial, the rest of the Yoga Mind practices begin with a moment or two of this breathing practice. If you like, you can also end your day this way, doing a few rounds of Deergha Swasam before you go to sleep. And of course, you can do this practice whenever you want to feel calmer and more relaxed.

✳

if you have breathing difficulties
or breathe with assistance

Breathing is the most natural thing in the world, until it isn't. Breathing can change or become limited due to illnesses or injuries. We've seen examples of assisted breathing in Stephen Hawking and Christopher Reeve, for whom ventilators became a necessary part of life. If this is the case for you, you can still do a pranayama practice.

Prana is the Sanskrit word for the life force, the energy that courses through all of us. One of the practices I learned in yoga teacher training was a meditation involving visualization of prana throughout the body. This is an especially useful meditation for people whose breathing is difficult or assisted. There are two ways to do prana meditation:

prana meditation with the breath

1. If it's comfortable for you to close your eyes, allow them to close gently. If you prefer to keep your eyes open, cast your gaze softly in front of you a few feet. Allow your breathing to be as it is—no need to try to manipulate or change it in any way. Let your awareness rest on your inhalation and exhalation, simply noting, without judgment, physical sensations associated with breathing, its sound, its rhythm. Allow your mind to relax by focusing gently on this nonjudgmental observation for a moment or two.

2. Next, bring to mind a vision of what pure energy might look like. This will be unique to you; your mind may become

very creative in imagining how energy might appear. View this energy in your mind, and hold it in your mind's eye. This is your prana.

3. Now, with each breath, see the prana moving throughout your body. You direct the prana. Send it from your mind to your throat and neck, across your collarbones to your shoulders, down through your arms, all the way to your fingertips. Go slowly. The prana is purely beneficial. There may be mild sensations as you move it through your body. Remember, this is your prana, your own personal life force, so you decide whether the prana feels warm or cool, tingles, vibrates, or is still, is soft, or has any discernible sensations.

4. Slowly move the prana back through your arms and into your chest, front and back; your abdomen and middle back, then lower back; your hips; and your legs, all the way down to your feet. Take your time. Then direct the prana to any area that needs extra attention.

5. When you feel complete with this meditation, bring the prana back to your mind. Release it gently, knowing you can bring it back whenever you want. Return your awareness to your breathing, and, if your eyes are closed, open them slowly.

pure prana meditation

If you would prefer a meditation without the focus on breathing, use the above instructions, skipping step 1 and starting with step 2. To come out of the meditation, count from one to ten slowly, opening your eyes as you go along.

day 3

ahimsa

(ah-HIM-sa)
Non-harming;
not causing pain to any living being,
including ourselves.

A himsa is one of a group of ethical principles known as the yamas, or behaviors to cultivate toward others. In yoga school, our teachers talked about living this ethical principle by being vegetarians, for obvious reasons. (When I was a child, I asked my nana where lamb chops came from. She thought for a moment before answering, "The butcher shop.") Less obvious are the subtle ways that we can harm others and ourselves, and the tricky ethical dilemmas that come up in the noble, nearly impossible pursuit of living a harm-free life.

A few weeks after Francesco did his first yoga practice with Three-Part Breathing, he was discharged from the hospital. He couldn't return to his apartment; he was completely dependent on others, twenty-four hours a day, for everything, including showering, dressing, being fed, even brushing his teeth. I had trouble imagining what it would be like to be a conscious, mature adult in a body that was more helpless than an infant's.

Francesco's life in Manhattan was packed up and moved back to his childhood home in a suburb of New York, where his parents and sister still lived. It was less than an hour from New York City, so when Fran told me he wanted to continue the yoga breath work sessions we'd been doing in the hospital, I happily said I'd come to him. We'd both been encouraged by the results of his practice, even this early on. (This was before studies had been published on the benefits of breathing exercises, along with asana and talk therapy, in reducing the effects of PTSD on war veterans.) The deep, relaxing Deergha Swasam breathing kept him calm during medical procedures that ranged from pain inducing to dignity stripping. It also helped, along with Fran's bellowing Madonna songs, to reinflate the lung that had collapsed when he was drowning in the pool. Over time, his damaged lung was restored to a pre-accident level of health.

Francesco wasn't the only one experiencing benefits. Meeting with him, and teaching him yoga tools, was relieving the despair of the helplessness I'd felt when I first saw him. Being of service brought balance to my life. I felt needed and useful. As I took the train from the city to the leafy suburbs, I remembered my sankalpa and added that I would meet with Francesco for as long as he wanted to keep doing yoga.

Fran was redefining what "doing yoga" meant. To me and almost everyone else I knew, doing yoga meant moving through a series of postures. I knew from my teacher training that there was more to yoga than just the physical exercises, but Francesco was becoming a living, deeply breathing illustration of that point. I was glad I'd never given his practice another name that might have imbued a sense of limitation. When Nonni led me into the living room, where Francesco lay on a large metal hospital bed, he signed off with someone on the phone by saying, "I have to go, I'm about to do yoga." I could hear a confused voice on the other end say, "You're doing *what*?" before Nonni hung up the phone for him.

"You didn't have to end the call on my account," I said after giving him a double cheek kiss, Italian style.

"I had to end it on my account," he said. He was partially propped up in the hospital bed, just one of the new additions to the Clarks' home. A wheelchair ramp now bridged the driveway and a side door; the front door had stairs and was now unusable for him, as was his childhood room on the second floor. A half bathroom off the kitchen had been renovated to accommodate a shower stall with a seat. "I just couldn't talk to that person anymore," he continued.

"Why?" I asked as I pulled one of the antique chairs near him and sat. Much of the living room furniture had been pushed aside to accommodate the mechanized hospital bed and a crane apparatus that hydraulically lifted Fran from the bed to the wheelchair. "What happened?"

Fran sighed. "People mean well. They're being really nice, offering to do whatever they can, bringing over food, asking how they can help. They want to talk to me and visit. But when they come over, their faces look like somebody died. And whether they're here or on the phone, they ask me a lot about the accident and what I'm going to do now. I don't really want to talk about the accident, and all my doctors say is that I'm never going to move again and I'd better get used to being in a wheelchair." The gravity of that statement made him pause. "So I try to talk to people about work, their families—you know, what's going on in their lives. They'll start talking, even grousing about their job or whatever, in a normal way. And then they say, 'Oh, but I shouldn't complain; after all, look at *you*.'" He sighed again, the big smile nowhere to be found in this new, modified room. "Just what I always wanted to be," he said, "everyone's worst-case scenario."

In times of trouble, such as a cancer diagnosis or a divorce or any type of sudden and potentially devastating news, most of us just don't know what to say. The people who were showing concern and offering to help Fran had the best of intentions; they simply didn't realize that their reactions might have an unintended yet still harmful effect on him. This was one of the lessons in the subtleties of ahimsa. We can cause harm without even realizing it.

Another lesson came just as we were having this discussion. Francesco's grandmother returned with two bowls of soup. This soup was one of the most fragrantly mouth-watering things that I have ever smelled in my life, and it was beautifully simple—rice topped with grated Parmesan cheese in a golden homemade chicken broth. Nonni offered me a bowl. I was still trying to follow my teachers' example of living ahimsa by being vegetarian, so I politely refused.

Only as Francesco translated my explanation to Nonni in Italian did I realize how tricky non-harming can be. Nonni's face took on the soft sadness of rejection. In a moment of such crystalline clarity that the edges could've cut me, I realized that this woman's life mission—what yogis would call her svadharma—was giving love to her family in the form of cooking. The helplessness that Nonni and the rest of Fran's family felt was mitigated only by what they could do to give him some comfort. Nonni had left her home in Italy and moved to a place where she didn't even have the language to ask at the supermarket where an item might be found, all so she could cook for her family—and her family's well-intentioned, but ignorant, visitor. In trying not to cause harm by eating an animal, I'd caused harm to an Italian grandmother. My karma was in the toilet.

Stupid, stupid, stupid, I thought to myself on the train ride home, until I saw yet another lapse in my practice of ahimsa. The definition is not causing pain to any living being, *including ourselves*. The ways we can hurt other people are usually fairly clear. Then there are ways that are less obvious, such as my refusing Nonni's food based on ethical principles. Subtler still are the ways in which we harm ourselves through negative self-talk, that unsupportive, demeaning inner dialogue. These are the voices in our heads that say we're not good enough, or thin enough, or attractive enough, or *whatever* enough. *I'm so fat, That was a dumb mistake, I'll never get anywhere in life, I don't look as good as I did when I was younger,* or the brief and powerful mother of them all, *I can't.* Whether the voices come from teachers or parents or we formed them ourselves, these opinions—don't confuse them with facts—can become so ingrained over time that we may barely notice them. But make no mistake, their cumulative damage can be crippling.

I began to pay more attention to my inner narrative and was unpleasantly surprised by how many subtly negative thoughts went through my mind in an average day. I criticized my body in the shower and when I got dressed; every meal's nutritional value, calorie count, and environmental impact; my work performance. It seemed as if everything I did was dragged before an inner judge and jury that always pronounced me guilty.

I was alarmed, but I held myself back from feeling like something was wrong with me. There was no sense in doubling the harm by beating myself up for having unsupportive thoughts. And there was every reason to take positive action, since I couldn't conjure up a single example of a berating thought leading to beneficial change.

When people became upset over seeing Francesco in his wheelchair, he changed the subject in a way that was gentle and deft. I decided to take the same approach. When I had a negative thought, it was mentally stamped *TBNT*—short for "Thanks, but no thanks." Then I would say something positive, or at least neutral. *My body is healthy. Everyone makes mistakes. I can accomplish anything. A smile is all I need to look good, at any age.* And the brief but powerful mother of them all, *I can.*

yoga mind practice:
Attitude Alignment with Ahimsa

Today you'll tune in to your inner dialogue and, if the messages are not supportive, begin cultivating a kinder and more loving tone.

This is different from listening to your intuition. Each of us comes equipped with an inner guidance system that, among other things, gives us warning of potential danger. This should be heeded. The thoughts we're working with here feel more like judgment, usually of yourself.

Start with your yoga breathing practice. Sit or lie down so that you're comfortable, your spine is lengthened, and you can breathe as easefully as possible. Follow the instructions in the Deergha Swasam practice from day two, and do a few rounds of three-part breathing. Then breathe at your own natural pace. Let your attention rest on your breathing. If your mind wanders, steer it gently back to your inhalation and exhalation.

After a moment or two of this calming practice, bring to mind any thoughts and feelings you have that accompany decisions and actions—the commentary that goes on inside your head. Are the thoughts observations, such as it's time to eat, or are they more judgmental, chiding you for what you choose to eat? Does fear come up often, keeping you from trying new things with threats of failure?

Make notes about the general tone of your thoughts in your Yoga Mind journal. You can write down individual thoughts, or give an overall assessment of whether they are supportive or negative. If nothing occurs to you right now, take your journal with you and jot down any observations you have about the tone of your thoughts as they occur throughout the day. Observe the thoughts without judgment; you're simply noticing and taking notes.

At the end of the day, see how often you encouraged yourself or discouraged yourself. Then, for any negative thoughts, write a positive version. For example, you could turn *I hate my thighs* into *My legs are strong and support me throughout my day*. You'll learn how to use more positive-language yoga tools such as mantra, or mind protection; Pratipaksha Bhavana, the Yoga Thought-Swap Trick; and japa, repeated mantra meditation, in coming chapters. For now, whenever negative thoughts arise, make them do a handstand with a shift toward positive, encouraging inner dialogue.

---

holding space: the three-minute listening exercise

Cheri Clampett is the founder of the Therapeutic Yoga training program, and she teaches yoga at the Cancer Center of Santa Barbara. Part of her Therapeutic Yoga training is teaching instructors that people who are going through health events want and need to talk about their conditions, but listeners often interrupt in an effort to comfort them. Sometimes, they say the wrong thing; most of the time, the person speaking doesn't really want advice, and definitely doesn't want to hear "Oh my God, how terrible!" They just want to speak, and to be heard.

This exercise, which I learned from Cheri and her co-teacher Arturo Peal when I took Therapeutic Yoga training, is designed to teach us how to do something very basic but incredibly valuable and generous: just listen.

Sit with a friend or partner. Set your phone or kitchen timer for three minutes and let your friend talk about their day, a life event, or whatever is currently on their mind. Your job is to listen for the full three minutes *without interrupting them*. You will be amazed at how difficult this can be. You'll want to say things like, "Yes, that happened to someone I know," and tell that story; you'll want to soothe them or tell them about a treatment you heard about or ask questions. It's part of our hardwiring as humans to connect with people. Yet a true and deep connection can be achieved by simply honoring people's desire to be heard.

So listen, without interruption of any kind. Then repeat back what the person said. You don't have to say it all word for word, but you'll know how deeply you were listening by how many details you can recall. Then switch, with you talking for three minutes and your partner listening.

mantra

(MAHN-tra)
A word or phrase repeated silently
to yourself to keep the mind focused
during meditation.

A man is but the product of his thoughts;
what he thinks, he becomes.
—Mahatma Gandhi

Mantra, we were told one day in yoga philosophy class, means "mind protection." Up until then I'd thought of mantra in the pop culture sense, as a sentence repeated to stave off stress, or something that you wanted to become deeply entrenched in your brain, like my *Take a deep breath* litany at work. But in yoga teacher training, Swami Asokananda translated *mantra* as "mind protection."

"Protection from what?" one of the students asked.

"All sorts of things," the swami said. "Everything from getting lost in the to-do list to more negative thoughts, like replaying a fight you had with someone, to worrying about what-if scenarios in some imagined future that may never happen. Those aren't the best objects of meditation," he said with a smile. "Words can affect us deeply. A mantra, whether it's in Sanskrit, English, or any other language, is made up of positive words that have beneficial vibrations. They can protect our minds from unskillful, even harmful thoughts."

Francesco had been forming his own mantra to protect his mind against thoughts that could cause as much harm as his injury, in different ways. As the weeks after his accident became months, he was entering a new phase, adjusting to each difficult, daunting aspect of his new life. A miraculous recovery seemed less and less likely. His doctors had words that affected Francesco deeply, and they repeated them over and over: *It's time to accept life in a wheelchair and move on.*

But what did "move on" mean, exactly? How was Fran supposed to move on—get a job, become independent again, even just use the bathroom by himself—when he couldn't move? For lack of any solid suggestions, *move on* seemed synonymous with practicing a depressing form of acceptance, where Fran was supposed to be satisfied with sitting in his wheelchair and staring out his window every day. To protect his mind against the negative connotations of *move on*, Francesco started saying, "When I get better."

This phrase began and ended his sentences, helping to support visions of the future that, while vague, were promising. *When I get better* was roomy enough for both optimism and realism. With a spinal cord injury as severe as his, walking fell into the category of miraculous. *Better* was nonspecific enough to allow for the unknown, which, in this case, was far preferable to the known. Occasionally Francesco would say, "When I can walk again," but mostly he focused on "When I get better." That mantra held him up straighter than the metal frame that allowed Fran to stand upright, strapped in to keep him from falling.

"I forgot how tall you are," I said, being careful not to say *were*. I didn't want to cut his life into two distinct pieces, *before* and *after*.

He laughed as he looked down at me, but then he suddenly grew pale. "Suz, Charlotte, I need you to massage my legs, ankles toward knees," he said. "My blood pressure's getting weird and I'm going to pass out." The accident had thrown most of his bodily functions out of whack, including blood pressure regulation; because of his lack of movement, his blood was draining from the top portion of his body and pooling in the lower portion. Fran's sister showed me how to literally press his blood back upward, toward his head.

"Whoo, thanks," he said as the color returned to his cheeks.

"Will that happen every time you're in an upright position?" I asked as Fran's aide and sister lowered him back to his bed.

"I'll be able to get my blood moving on my own with different kinds of exercise machines," Fran explained, "when I get better."

Eventually, through participation in clinical trials on spinal cord injuries, Francesco did get on those machines. Muscle by recovered muscle, nerve by partial nerve, he regained some upper-body mobility and used it to propel his limbs forward and back in a simulated walking motion. This movement came from his willingness to try any treatment, including receiving mild electrical shocks in his brain and having additional surgery on his neck. But it all started with the belief ingrained in his mind with the simple mantra *When I get better.*

Science has only recently proven what yogis knew thousands of years ago: our thoughts can affect our bodies. An article published by the University of Minnesota reported that stress from negative thoughts and feelings adversely affects hormonal balance and the immune system, and could even affect a person's life span by shortening telomeres, the part of DNA strands associated with aging. The benefit of positive thoughts includes stronger immunity, faster healing, improved sleep, and greater emotional resilience.

It's easy to see how being positive would be the obvious choice when speaking theoretically, but it's difficult to put into practice when you or someone close to you is facing a life trauma—a major illness, dealing with aging parents suffering from dementia, the end of a job or a relationship, or similar emotionally jarring events. Additionally, we've been told so much about the adverse effects of everyday stress that when atypically stressful events occur, there's almost a rush to avoid or end pain. That doesn't let us get *through* pain by allowing for feelings entirely appropriate to these situations. Must we always turn that frown upside down so fast?

Yogic thinking would say no. A person's satya, or truth, should be honored. Healthy emotional stages allow for honest acknowledgment of shock, anger, sadness, then acceptance and reorientation, and, eventually, an openness toward the unknown—which can also be thought of as possibilities.

This was what Francesco did. He understood that spinal cord injuries don't have an encouraging recovery rate, but he also opted to focus on possibilities, in a realistic, optimistic way: *When I get better*. With a mantra like that, he would only keep improving.

yoga mind practice:
Creating Your Own Personal Mantra

When going through formal yoga training, students can request a mantra from a teacher after a period of dedicated study. But we all have access to mind-protecting thoughts through the better-known avenue of affirmations. A mantra doesn't have to be in an ancient language to work; in fact, it's more likely to be beneficial if you understand what you're saying.

Your mantra can be general, as Francesco's was, and be more effective than something specific. A mantra such as *I want to lose fifteen pounds* can take on a frustrating tone, whereas *I am fit, healthy, and beautiful* sounds, well, wonderful! Note the difference between *I will* and *I am*. Yoga doesn't deal with imagined "someday" futures that may never come. It takes place in the present moment, where, as Dr. Wayne Dyer said when he echoed Gandhi's statement, "As you think, so shall you be."

Even if you don't completely believe your mantra at first, that's okay. The very reason you're creating it is so you can *achieve* that state of being. The more you state your mantra, whether aloud or silently, the more new neural pathways you create in your brain. Think of them as new paths leading you toward positive possibilities.

To create your personal mantra, choose an area of your life you would like to strengthen and support or a quality you would like to cultivate. A few examples:

I am becoming more my true self every day.

I embody compassion.

I am a channel of love and kindness.

I am a divine light.

Sit comfortably and close your eyes. Begin your Deergha Swasam three-part breathing practice and continue for a few slow rounds. Allow your mind to grow calm and your personal mantra to form. When you have one that feels right to you, write it in your Yoga Mind journal and commit to saying it to yourself when you wake up, at midday, and before you go to bed for the duration of this course. Chances are good that you'll want to say it even more as you begin to feel its effects.

day 5

dharana

(DAR-ana)
Concentration;
focusing the mind;
the starting point of meditation.

My weekly meetings with Francesco became a calming routine we both looked forward to. We'd catch up over tea and Nonni's homemade sugar cookies, and then he would let everyone in the house know we were going to do yoga so that we would not be interrupted. We began with my leading Fran through the steps for Deergha Swasam breathing. After a few rounds I would instruct him to let his breathing follow its own natural rhythm. Then we would do the prana meditation, with Fran's focus on sending the prana energy he brought in with each inhalation to help heal his spine.

Our guided meditations started at five minutes, then went to ten, sometimes even fifteen minutes or longer. His ability to keep his awareness on his breathing was admirable, his concentration fixed but not strained. For the entire time—and fifteen minutes can be a long stretch of beach—our attention remained on one thing: the gentle waves of breathing.

I wonder if we would be able to do this today.

Fran and I were doing this practice at a time before smartphones and social media alerts and texts and emails that *ping!* during movies and meditation sessions alike. Today, it's not unusual for me to see students checking their phones not only before yoga classes but during the class, in between poses. Even if they've silenced the phones, they feel that mental pull to check, check, check: Did someone from work email? Did their friend text about meeting up? Back when all cell phones could do was ring annoyingly during deep relaxation, I asked students to turn them off, and they did. Later, when smartphones could do anything from get your email to find a restaurant and tell you that someone on Facebook liked your post, students put them on vibrate, but they didn't turn them off. They just didn't seem to be able to.

The other yoga teachers and I knew that some of our students couldn't disconnect from work that seemed to have no end time, so we just asked them to silence the phones. Although the phones wouldn't ring or ping or buzz during class, people still kept checking, more than could possibly have had work or family emergencies. They simply couldn't get away from that pull to *check, check, check.* The result was that they couldn't quite bring their attention to their bodies and minds so they could de-stress—the very reason they'd come to yoga in the first place.

With the advent of living with and by technology that pulls our attention in so many different directions, we're only beginning to understand the effects on our ability to concentrate. We fall victim to the myth of multitasking, believing we can have a conversation on the phone while writing an email and eating lunch. Multitasking was something humans engineered computers to do, but they also began applying the theory to themselves in an effort to be more productive.

I could never seem to get it to work. I ended up with a lot of things half-done half-correctly; I made mistakes and got mustard on my work. The reason multitasking didn't work for me, and doesn't really work for anyone, came from Julie Morgenstern, the bestselling organizational and time-management expert I met while working at *The Oprah Magazine*. "Our brains are wired for monotasking, giving our undivided attention to a task," she told me. "When we switch back and forth between several things, it can take the brain four times longer to recognize and process what it was working on—'Where was I? What was I doing?' The prefrontal cortex is working overtime to get it all figured out; that creates stress, and that sets off cortisol, the fight-or-flight stress hormone." The result is that feeling of burnout, and over time, this can even lead to memory problems.

Another reason for the decline in our ability to focus is known as the dopamine loop. Dopamine is a neurotransmitter (a kind of chemical messenger) in the brain that helps us think, sleep, and make controlled movements, among other things. It's also the inner gearshift that puts us in *drive* to search for food, a partner, and information. Once we get whatever dopamine had us looking for, we get a rush of satisfaction—*Yesss!*—but only for a short time. Then dopamine has us searching for another cupcake, another book, another date, another new pair of shoes, more news, more social media posts. This genius engineering in our brains was designed to keep our hunting, gathering ancestors searching for more and varied things to eat, thereby maximizing their chances of survival.

Although finding food isn't difficult for most of us these days, being able to focus on one thing at a time is a challenge and a half. Remember, dopamine is just as interested in seeking out potentially valuable information as it is in food. The Internet, with its seemingly endless amount of information, provides dopamine with more and more opportunities to seek, more instant gratification, and endless opportunities to hunt for more. And while the Web used to be accessible to us only through computers, it's now available to us all the time via our smartphones. Did that email come through? *Let's find out!* says dopamine. Did anyone text me? How many likes did I get on my Facebook post? *Check to see*, says dopamine, *check, and check again*. The brain gets its rush of satisfaction, and when that fizzles out, it wants another. The more it gets, the more it wants. Over time, the brain becomes like a child turned loose in a candy store, running around in all different directions, wanting more and different and new.

As far as our ability to focus is concerned, the combination of multitasking and the dopamine loop is a marriage made in hell.

In its least harmful form, you and your partner gaze unblinkingly into laptops or your phones while a movie plays on your flat-screen, and when the evening's done you're not quite sure what you posted or watched, or where that bag of chips went because you don't remember eating them. At its worst, the pairing is deadly. In 2013, according to a report from the Centers for Disease Control and Prevention, 424,000 people were injured in car crashes that resulted from distracted driving, which is defined as using a phone, texting, and/or eating while driving. (The report notes that GPS systems can also distract drivers.) That same year, 3,154 people were killed in distracted-driving crashes.

Remember when we used to just drive? Just watch a movie? Just eat and talk? I remember when Francesco and I used to just focus on our breathing: Inhaling. Exhaling. Watching the waves come, go, and come again, in that soothing rhythm of life. As Francesco observed his breathing, his mind was calmed, and his body was able to resume its healing process when the sympathetic nervous system's stress response was reduced and the parasympathetic nervous system took over. This process could not have happened without his consciously placing his attention on one thing: his breathing.

Yoga's name for this gentle focus is dharana. Thousands of years ago, when people were trying to learn how to meditate, yoga's wise practitioners told their students about dharana, the beginning stages of meditation. Just focus. Train your attention on one thing. Not in a way that makes you strain or become frustrated. Simply bring your focus to an object to meditate

on, like the one that accompanies you like a dear friend everywhere—your own breathing.

yoga mind practice:
Strengthen Dharana One Breath at a Time

By increasing our ability to focus, we become more effective. We
get more done, and we do it better. We can absorb information
better, thereby helping us to make more informed decisions. We
enjoy things more. Overall, we no longer feel what one of my
students described: "Life is passing me by, and I have no idea
where it went." The ability to focus can enhance every area of
your life and every relationship.

The first step to meditating, even before dharana, is to
release any preconceived ideas that you may have about meditation. The one I hear most often from students? "I can't clear my
mind." You don't have to. Nor do you need to climb to a serene
mountaintop or have other "perfect" conditions; I meditate
every day in a noisy city, and I particularly enjoy meditating on
the subway. And no, you don't have to give up your smartphone.

You *will* have to silence your phone and leave it in another
room, though, unless you're using it to time this practice. In that
case, place it facedown a few feet away from you, so you're not
tempted to peek at it.

For today's practice in strengthening dharana, or focus, use
your breathing as the object of your meditation. Begin with a few
rounds of your Deergha Swasam three-part breathing practice,

and then allow your breathing to find its own natural rhythm, focusing all the while on your inhalation and your exhalation. You don't have to breathe too deeply or at any particular pace; let your body breathe the way it wants to. You're not trying to change it, just being aware of it.

Your mind *will* wander. That's what it was designed to do, but not in the ways it does today, reliving the past, creating future scenarios, or getting a dopamine rush from exciting things on our phones. You're just breathing now. Breathing is pretty miraculous, if you take the time to notice it. You've got all these muscles around your chest, between each and every rib, and your diaphragm is working in a symphony of expansion and contraction to accommodate air. Your lungs take in oxygen and remove carbon dioxide from your body with the help of the alveoli, tiny grape-shaped clusters that bring oxygen to your blood each time you breathe. Did you know there are approximately *six hundred million* of these little alveoli guys in your lungs? I didn't, until I learned about it in the anatomy and physiology course in yoga teacher training. After that, I found my breathing to be a fascinating subject for meditation.

So when your mind wanders, gently bring your attention back to your inhalation . . . your exhalation . . . that space when one becomes the other. Do this as many times as you need to. As you'll learn in an upcoming chapter, returning to your focus *is* meditation. Try this breathing-focused meditation for two minutes.

Your second dharana practice today is to choose one thing that you will focus on from start to finish, without distraction. Here's an easy one: eating. When it's time for lunch, just eat your lunch.

Don't work while eating, or go online, or talk on the phone, or write emails, or, you guessed it, get lost in your phone. Here's what you do: enjoy your meal! Hopefully you'll get something you like, which makes it easier to focus on it. Before you begin eating, take a moment to give thanks. At Integral Yoga, everyone who is having lunch together, including the people who prepared the food, gathers to sing a meal prayer that gives thanks for everything and everyone involved in bringing the meal to the table. You don't have to sing in Sanskrit to give thanks. If you have a traditional prayer you use in your family, say that. Or just bring to mind a sense of gratitude for this meal before you.

Next, take a moment to notice the aroma, the colors, the textures, the various ingredients. With your first bite, notice the flavors, the sensations. Eat slowly; savor.

I confess that I'm as guilty as anyone when it comes to the working lunch, ramming food down my gullet and barely noticing what I'm eating as I type away at the computer. But when I take the time to do a dharana lunch, the difference is remarkable: I feel *satisfied*. I also eat less afterward, because I've really enjoyed the meal. I feel that I've rightly honored the gift of the food; when my nana was a teenager, she and her family had so little to eat during the Great Depression that they suffered from malnutrition. Food is a blessing. Honoring meals with gratitude is another way for me to cultivate happiness during my day, as well as strengthen my ability to focus.

Note your feelings about your dharana practices, both breathing and your meal, in your Yoga Mind journal. Choose another thing tomorrow to focus on, and another the next day, and so on.

what is mindfulness?

Mindfulness and *awareness* are two words often associated with meditation. Both can mean bringing your attention to something, purposefully but without brow-furrowing, gritted-teeth, laser-beams-shooting-out-of-your-eyes focus. Mindfulness just means giving something you're doing your full attention. Knitters working intently on their stitches know this feeling, as do painters, sculptors, or anyone who does intricate work with their hands.

Awareness is more about taking note of something, not necessarily an action. For example, right now, bring your awareness to your feet by feeling whatever they're next to— your socks, the insides of your shoes, the floor. Do your feet feel warm? Cool? Snug in their socks or shoes? Small movements can help you receive more information. Wiggle your toes, shift your feet slightly, lift your heels and set them down again. Awareness can become a meditation in itself, noting how your body feels part by part, as long as it's unaccompanied by judgment. This is the difference between noting *My feet are cold* and *My feet are cold because I shouldn't have worn these shoes, they're pretty but they weren't right for this weather, darn it, why didn't I wear my ugly rain boots . . .* See the difference?

Awareness can also be a tool that helps change a state of being. In yoga nidra, the deep relaxation part of a yoga class, we instruct students to bring awareness to each part of the body and mentally ask it to relax completely. Becoming aware of each part brings about a deeper, more conscious state of relaxation. Yoga nidra is a very beneficial form of reducing stress; I give instructions for it in the practice for day seven, and also on my website at http://suzancolon.net/yoga-nidra-instructions/.

We hear a lot that we should be more mindful in everything that we do, but there are times when you might be better off *not* being so mindful. I know, spiritual sacrilege—a yoga teacher telling you not to bring your awareness fully to something! But there are specific times when I make a deliberate choice not to be mindful: during medical procedures, such as dental surgery, mammograms, and gynecological exams.

These routine procedures are uncomfortable. There are many more medical procedures that, while beneficial, are far more painful. There are people who use painful experiences as a way to deepen their meditation, but for me, I get through treatments far more easily, and with a sense of time passing quickly, by directing my awareness elsewhere. I believe that whatever created us gave us the power of imagination for many good reasons, including the ability to get through a mammogram without becoming unhinged. When I know that some degree of pain will be involved, it's *mindfulness, schmindfulness*. I'll listen to a guided meditation, or, if a device isn't allowed (as with MRIs), I use my imagination to replay a favorite movie or make up a new one. I return to full attention when the doctor gives me the assessment or instructions afterward.

We've all been given the gift of imagination. We can dream, invent stories and images, travel back in time, and create the kind of future we want for ourselves. The point is not to stay there. People escape from realities they don't like by spending too much time in their own creative imaginations, but that means we'll never do the real-world work to realize our dreams.

Overall, we should be mindful, paying attention to each moment of our very real lives. That can include focusing on the root canal your dentist is doing in your mouth if that works for you. If not, consider this your permission slip to be unmindful during that time.

sangha

(SAHNG-ha)
A group of like-minded people,
usually walking the same spiritual path.

My friends, family, and coworkers asked about Francesco constantly. I told them about his strong optimism and his mantra of *When I get better*, but the yoga part took more explaining. I tried to make them understand that we weren't doing a *physical* practice, that I wasn't twisting his body into poses. We were meditating and breathing. "Oh," they'd say. And then, "Do you think that will help?"

I didn't know.

I was very careful not to make promises to Fran about any kind of results, choosing instead to stay in the action. For someone being told that nothing more can be done, an action in itself is helpful. It was *something*.

But what kind of something, we didn't know. People who

love yoga think yoga can cure anything, and in a way, they're right—it can cure fear, which affects everything. But yoga, whether physical or spiritual, wasn't going to make Fran able to walk overnight. Whether I was working with Francesco or sharing updates with people concerned about him, I tried to maintain as neutral a form of optimism as possible.

This was difficult when the story of Fran's accident triggered fear in people—"Oh my God, that's *horrible*! If that happened to me, I would want to die!" In those cases, I would try to comfort the person, which wasn't easy without negating their feelings ("No, you wouldn't") or painting a Pollyanna picture of Fran's experiences ("He's okay—almost completely paralyzed, but otherwise great!"). Either way, I had a lot of conversations where I had to be the calm presence, which meant I had limited support to help me deal with my own fearful feelings.

This is how a sangha differs from a group of friends. A sangha is a community of people who gather together for a purpose, because they're walking the same spiritual path or they're supporting one another through an event. A cancer support group is a sangha; a twelve-step group is a sangha; a Buddhist meditation group is a sangha; a Bible study group is a sangha; a yoga teacher training is a sangha. A sangha can be comprised of friends, or it can be made up of strangers who form a close bond by sharing a common thread. They provide support for one another in a way that even close family and friends might not be able to, because they understand each other.

The beneficial effects of community go deep. The Mayo Clinic reports that support groups reduce stress, as well as improve skills in coping with divorce, job loss, the death of someone close, or other trauma. Close friendships can reduce stress and increase confidence and feelings of self-worth.

Had I been in yoga teacher training after Francesco's accident, I would have had a sangha for support in processing my own feelings of shock about what had happened to him and my occasional trepidation about our yoga sessions. I believed in yoga's ability to help him in some way; my doubts were about *my* ability to help him. But I'd just graduated from yoga teacher training, so I was on my own, without that group of like-minded yogis and regular meetings with my teachers to rely on.

Still, I had a few steady-as-rocks friends who saw that I needed support, like Marnie. She could ask about Francesco and not go bonkers with existential angst. She would listen—just listen—and then ask, "How are you doing with all of this?"

"It's your birthday, Marn," I said one night when we'd gone out to dinner with a few friends. "We're supposed to be celebrating you, not talking about me."

"I asked," she countered. "Tell me how you're doing, or no soft-shelled crabs sautéed in butter for you." She knew exactly how to get to me. We'd been as close as sisters almost from the day we'd met while working at the same magazine. Even though she was now a rock star in the publicity department of a major fashion company, hanging out with supermodels and traveling all over America and Europe, every couple of days I'd pick up the phone and hear her trilled greeting of "Suz!" (My automatic reply: "Marn!") Whenever I started a new job, I'd arrive to find a tasteful bouquet of flowers on my new desk from her—"So they'll know you're important." Marnie made everyone feel important. In times of confusion about my career, relationships, and now trying to help Francesco, Marnie was the earth, solid and sustaining.

And now, even though the focus should've been on the birthday girl, I unloaded about my fears that I might be offering Francesco some sort of false hope through our yoga practice and my doubts about my ability to help him. Marnie didn't make the conversation about her reactions. She didn't say much, and in fact it was her steady listening that did more to help me regain a sense of stability than any advice she could have given.

I stopped talking when the soft-shelled crabs came to the table in all their buttery glory. Marnie, a near-chef-level cook who knew all the best restaurants in Manhattan, loved food. Tonight, though, after eating, she winced and gripped the edge of the table with white-knuckled pain.

The rest of us paused with forks in midair, alarmed, asking her what was wrong. After a moment, Marnie released a tight breath. "Just some weird indigestion," she said. "Probably the upcoming fashion show giving me an ulcer or something. Okay, emergency over—dessert, now!" And with her typical graciousness, Marnie went back to asking everyone else about their lives, focusing on her friends at her own birthday party.

I sat back and admired the ease with which Marnie moved through life. I wished I could be as confident as she was, but I was just grateful she was part of my sangha.

yoga mind practice:
Forming a Sangha

Friends and family are the marrow of life. They love us and want the best for us. Yet in some situations, they may not be able to relate to something that you're going through or that you want to do. That's where a sangha can be very helpful.

Support can come in many different types to suit your needs. Workouts are easy to cancel on rainy days, but you're more likely to show up if you have a group you work out with at the gym. In yoga teacher trainings, the students support one another when studying for exams, or when the training becomes daunting. I've seen many a trainee consider quitting and then decide to hang in there after getting support from the sangha of students.

In addition to providing support, sanghas help foster success. In a study done by Gail Matthews, PhD, a psychologist and career coach at Dominican University of California, a group of people who wrote down their goals (as you did with your sankalpa) and then shared them with another person had a greater success rate than the group that didn't, with 76 percent accomplishing their goals.

Of course there are also support groups that help people deal with the deeper emotional needs that accompany cancer treatment, grief and trauma, post-traumatic stress, recovery from addiction, and so on. If you're in one of those categories, you will benefit greatly from joining a group of people who understand what you're going through and will support your process. You can find one by calling your local hospital's patient services center (you don't need to be a patient to ask for information).

Whatever kind of life change you want to make, know that it can be easier and richer when done with a group of like-minded people who will share the journey with you—even if those friends are online. If you want some like-minded friends who are working this thirty-day program, visit my Spiritual Surfer Sangha group on Facebook. Share your sankalpa with us, and let us cheer you on.

brahmacharya

(brah-ma-CHAR-ee-ah)
Conservation of energy for the
pursuit of spiritual goals.

In yoga teacher training sessions, this discussion always triggered the giggles.

Brahmacharya is one of the five ethical principles, or yamas, to cultivate toward others, and the swamis, bless their material-world-renouncing hearts, explained it bluntly: "Brahmacharya means conservation of sexual energy."

Giggle. Giggle giggle giggle. This was a bit like hearing a parent or a clergy member talk about sex. The trainees couldn't imagine this person ever *having* sex, so how could they talk about it as something that you should refrain from as part of a spiritual practice? The swamis would patiently smile and wait for the giggles and random muttered comments of "No way" and "My husband won't go for that!" to subside. Then they explained a little further.

When yoga was being created thousands of years ago, it was a life path not unlike joining a convent, but the people joining or being enrolled were young men and boys. (In that time, it was not the practice for women to renounce their lives to take up a spiritual path.) Because these young men came to their teachers at an age when they'd normally be very interested in young women, their teachers had to impress them with the benefits of chastity, which included increased spiritual power. That was a much bigger cause for bragging rights in these circles than having a girlfriend, which would've been viewed as being a slacker.

"You have to understand, this was a long, long time ago," the swami explained to our group of trainees. "Though brahmacharya is still pretty useful today. We get a lot of young people here at the ashram who want to train to be yoga instructors, so even though we're like monks and nuns, we hear about what's going on with dating today. It seems like a lot of energy goes into figuring out whether you're actually dating because you hooked up, or whether you're friends or friends with benefits, all that stuff," the swami said to the now-nodding group. "It can really take you away from your life goals." The students, starting to understand this brahmacharya thing, would agree that, for the duration of their four months in yoga teacher training, they might calm down on the dating a little so they could study and pass their final exams.

For the married people, and people who were not in relationships at the time, brahmacharya translated into something similar and applicable: conservation not just of sexual energy but of prana—the life force, that vital energy in all living or natural things, from people to electricity. Prana is the force (some *Star Wars* fans in teacher trainings equated it with the Force) that makes all things go—or stop, when you don't have enough of it. That seems to happen more and more these days.

When asked the question "How are you?" we used to answer "Fine." In the last ten or so years, possibly alongside the increasing rise of technology that allows us the dubious benefit of always being connected to work, the answer became "Busy," then "Crazed," and now the efficiently doubled "Crazy busy." Some of what goes on in our lives is beyond our control, of course—work is work, newborns need to be fed. The yoga tool of brahmacharya becomes most useful to us when we choose to expend our energy in ways that aren't always beneficial to us or anyone else. One example: drama.

When I was working with Francesco, I was juggling a part-time office job and at-home freelance work for multiple clients. I was glad to have the work, and it allowed me the flexibility to see Francesco. I was also studying and teaching yoga, and I tried to see my friends on a regular basis. All this felt like a full, rich life. But I was also in a relationship that was *that* relationship— the emotional roller-coaster ride. It was adoring and confusing and on again and off again and full of drama that I reframed as romantic. I thought it must be a passionate love affair if we said, on a fairly regular basis, *I love you but I don't know if I can deal with you.*

Yep, this took up a lot of energy.

I devoted a great deal of my energy to tending to, thinking about, and trying to navigate (and yes, control) the relationship because I thought all that energy proved the depth of my love. Without meaning to, I also got to enjoy a fair bit of martyrdom among my female friends, though even they became weary of the soap opera–like slog of it all and eventually said, "You know, you could leave him. Did you ever think about that? Maybe you should." But wasn't this what Great Love Affairs were made of, trouble and an almost demented level of dedication? "Relationships are *supposed* to be work!" I told my boyfriend during one of our frequent no-win discussions.

"No, they're not," he said with an uncharacteristic calmness that came from rational thinking. "Relationships are supposed to be a refuge—from job stress, from the troubles of the world, from fear of getting old and sick and the big questions that have no answers. That's what relationships are supposed to be. A comfort, not another source of trouble."

Truth goes directly to your heart, whether you like it or not. It would be a neat end to the story to say that I agreed, wished him well, and left, but I'm human and I didn't, and neither did he. I hung on, not stubbornly, because that would've been a giant step up from where I was, but stupidly, and so did he, and we tormented each other for quite a while longer. More than a few times, I showed up for one of my meetings with Francesco with an emotional hangover from another night of fighting to save something that really needed to be released. The only benefit was that it turned the tables so Fran could have the chance to be of help to me instead of being helped all the time.

Learning about brahmacharya made me look at how I spent the precious resource of my energy and ask whether this was what relationships, and life overall, were supposed to be about. Should I really feel drained and emotionally spent all the time? I understood being worn out for a period of time; typically, the yoga teacher trainees would get to the three-quarter point of the training and, exhausted from trying to balance study with the rest of their lives, say they had to quit. Their teachers would remind them that they only had a few weeks to go, the sangha would give support, and the trainees would rally like marathoners with the finish line in sight. But open-ended energy drains are unsustainable. Something had to give.

I began to examine the individual parts of life that make a whole sense of being and living fully. I weighed what I gave, what replenished me so that I still had something to give, and what took (and took, and took) and didn't give back. My jobs put a roof over my head and food on my table, and they allowed me to do what I loved as a career. My work with Francesco gave me purpose; it felt like a defining moment, a gift of an opportunity to become the kind of person I'd always hoped to be. Plus Francesco was fun to hang out with. Yoga filled the well. Evenings with friends who energized me with their positivity, and who felt equally energized by me, stayed. Going out for drinks just for the sake of going out was, well, out, replaced by evenings in with healthy meals and an early bedtime that made me feel like the human equivalent of orange juice the next day.

As for the relationship, my boyfriend and I had a calm, compassionate discussion. We weren't quite ready to let go completely, and there had been no deal-breaking event that would justify a permanent breakup. Maybe we were just putting off the inevitable, but I wasn't looking for any more turbulence at the moment. We opted to take a break and focus our energy on our individual lives, grateful for the space, comforted by knowing that we were each a phone call away.

yoga mind practice:
Recharging Your Batteries with Brahmacharya

Sunday used to be known as the day of rest. But how often do you actually *rest* on your day of rest? Downtime has become such a rare and valuable commodity that, paradoxically, we end up filling it with things we want to do. It's not unusual for me to find myself on a Sunday afternoon surrounded by books, my yoga mat, a sketch pad and pens, a list of shows I want to watch, and the newspaper, and then thinking I should do a load of laundry . . . Before I know it, I've used up all my downtime and I don't feel rested at all.

Now I dedicate a block of time on Sunday afternoons to resting—*just* resting. Think you're getting enough rest when you go to bed at night? I'm willing to bet you'd admit you're not getting enough sleep. Also, yogic sages had an interesting take on sleep: sometimes, it's not all that restful. Dreams, even pleasurable ones, can be stimulating, and your body will react to the movies your mind is creating as though you were actually going through the experience. If you're stressed out and have anxiety dreams, you'll likely wake up feeling not very rested at all.

In yoga classes, there is a period at the end of the asana practice called yoga nidra, or deep relaxation. Most times it's brief, sometimes as short as three minutes. In Integral Yoga classes, we were taught that yoga nidra should last for fifteen minutes. This true downtime allows your sympathetic nervous system to relax and your parasympathetic nervous system to take over. During that time, your body functions at normal, healthy levels. After that period of rest, students feel ultra-relaxed and refreshed. Some fall asleep, and that's okay, but if you can remain awake, conscious but relaxed, yoga nidra can be a form of meditation.

Today, or on a day this weekend when you can relax undisturbed for fifteen minutes, try yoga nidra. Read through the instructions first. Then set a timer for fifteen minutes; if using your phone's timer, put calls, texts, and all other notifications on silent, rather than vibrate, and choose a soothing alarm sound.

Lie on your bed, the couch, or a yoga mat. Place a rolled-up towel under your knees to relax your lower back and a folded towel under your head to release your neck muscles.

1. Briefly tighten your leg muscles and flex your feet, then allow them to relax completely.

2. Tighten your arm muscles, make fists, splay your fingers, then relax your arms.

3. Take a deep breath, hold for a second, then let the air gush out through your mouth. Breathe naturally.

4. Let your head rock gently and slowly from side to side, releasing any tension from your neck muscles, and let your head find its own natural center.

5. Scrunch all your facial muscles toward your nose and release.

6. Make any other adjustments that will allow you to feel completely relaxed.

7. As you've done during pranayama meditation, allow your awareness to rest on your breathing. When your mind wanders, gently steer it back to your inhalation and your exhalation. Notice how relaxing this is.

8. When your alarm sounds, begin a few rounds of Deergha Swasam breathing, feeling each of the three parts of your inhalation and exhalation. Then bring your arms overhead and give yourself a nice deep full-body stretch.

day 8

asana

(AH-sa-na)
Practicing physical postures
with awareness and a balance of
effort and ease to revitalize
the body.

If you think of yoga as a tree, there are eight limbs that are considered the core elements: the yamas, or ethical attitudes we cultivate toward others to enhance relationships; the niyamas, or personal habits for optimal living; pranayama, the breathing practices; pratyahara, training your senses not to be distracted by the outer world so you can focus on your inner world; dharana, or concentration, the beginning stages of meditation; dhayana, a steady flow of attention; samadhi, knowing that you're one with all (a big achievement!); and asana, the physical practice.

To be honest, asana felt to me to be out of place in a story about a friend who became paralyzed. Also, this book focuses on the kind of yoga you can do anywhere, not just the kind that can be done on the mat. And there are already more than enough books about yoga poses. Yet leaving out one of yoga's eight main limbs also seemed off balance, and including a chapter on the importance of caring for the body gave me a chance to share a revelation that expanded my concept of a physical practice. This revelation came, as they do, with a plague of frogs.

I met my husband, Nathan, on a yoga retreat. During the weeklong trip, we discovered that we both loved *Star Trek*, comic book movies, cats, and lots of other things, especially yoga. So, when we got married two years later, we planned a yoga honeymoon.

The weather in Hawaii was balmy, the yoga retreat tropically gorgeous. The lodging was somewhat rustic, and we wondered why there was a nearly empty half gallon of vodka in the back of our closet. In a beautiful, serene yoga retreat, who would need to drink that heavily, and not even in one of the fun bars in town but in the room? Mysterious. We tossed the plastic jug in the recycling bin and went to feast on a dinner of fresh veggies and fish caught nearby. We toasted each other with pineapple juice as we watched the setting sun paint the sky in joyous oranges and reds.

And then we heard the first chirp.

Imagine a grasshopper chirping through a whistle into Spinal Tap's mountain of speakers. We heard this sound once, then again, and again and again as darkness fell, hundreds of deafening chirps. This, we were told, was the nocturnal mating call of the coqui frog. These tiny critters are native to Puerto Rico, where they live far off in the mountains and their music is part of the local folklore. Apparently a few coquis made a voyage in shipping containers to Hawaii, where they enjoyed their own honeymoon every night. Free from natural predators, they were fruitful and multiplied. Dozens, even scores were right outside our room, chirping at mega-volumes. No wonder the previous occupants had swilled vodka from a jug—they were driven mad by the all-night *yoo-hoo* of these amorous amphibians.

After three sleep-deprived nights, Nathan and I left our island paradise-turned-purgatory and went to a retreat in the very quiet Berkshires. And this, post–frog plague, was where the revelation came.

During one of the relaxing, restorative yoga classes, our teacher told us to keep our movements to what felt good and right for us that day. "We think yoga is about achieving specific poses, but if your body's not built a certain way and you can't do a crazy back bend, does that mean you're not doing yoga? No," she said as an older woman nodded with relief. "Yoga is the union of the body and the mind," the teacher continued. "Whatever your movement, move with awareness and focus. Any movement done mindfully can be yoga."

Any movement done mindfully can be yoga.

This reminded me of something my teachers at Integral Yoga always said: "Bring the pose to the student, rather than bringing the student to the pose." This made yoga's asanas accessible to people of all abilities.

And what of people like Francesco, who couldn't move? To enlarge his meditation and breathing practice, I'd begun talking him through an abbreviated asana series, instructing him to visualize bringing his hands together at his heart and following with a round of Surya Namaskaram, the Sun Salutation, instructed as though he were doing the physical practice.

This visualized practice wasn't just a way to placate him. A study by the Cleveland Clinic Foundation in Ohio compared two groups of average people; one group went to the gym and actually worked out, and the second group visualized, or imagined, a workout. Predictably, the group that did physical exercise had muscle increase, about 30 percent—yet so did the visualization group. They gained *nearly half as much muscle*, 13.5 percent, simply by *imagining* their workouts.

This is the power of the mind-body connection.

After reading that statistic and hearing that yoga instructor's freeing perception of an asana practice, I felt that yoga could help people in ways that I could only begin to imagine. The use of meditation and breathing practices helped people focus their minds, and that focus could in turn affect their physical health, not only by reducing stress but by increasing the effect of movement and by making yoga more available to people of different abilities.

And what timing. Over the past few decades, the collective health of Western nations has been sucker-punched by one surprising universal factor: we sit too much. Sitting for six or more hours a day can increase your risk of dying within fifteen years by an alarming *40 percent*. It increases the risk of gaining weight, which then tips the scales toward the possibility of developing diabetes, kidney malfunction, even cancer. How? Sitting burns 50 less calories per hour than standing, enzymes that break down fat drop by a chilling 90 percent, and it's a domino effect from there. The average American sits for over *nine* hours a day, at the office, commuting to and from work, and logging couch hours binge-watching Netflix.

One of my teachers, Chandra Jo Sgammato, said something to me once that had the clear ring of a life mission: "I believe that yoga can save the world." From the time that statement embedded itself in my heart, I looked for ways to prove it. What I learned about focus and physical movement, especially while working with Francesco, supplied one of the ways: any movement done mindfully is yoga.

yoga mind practice:
Find Your Yoga

Whether you have a daily physical practice of some kind, you intend to exercise but usually don't, or your physical movement is limited, there is a form of yoga for you. The key is remembering that any movement done mindfully can be thought of as yoga— the union of mind, body, and breath. By bringing focus to your movements, even movements that are visualized, you can create your own asana practice, no matter your age, fitness level, or physical condition.

If you already have a physical practice, whether yoga asana or another kind, begin today to bring mindfulness to your movement. At the gym, throw a towel over the screen on the treadmill or stationary bike and bring your attention to how the movement makes you feel, physically and mentally.

And you don't have to limit mindfulness to your workout routine. If you work at a desk, set an alarm to go off every hour to remind you to move, and take a mindful walk around your office. You can also download my iTunes app, Take a Yoga Break, which has a series of yoga-based movements you can do right at your desk.

If you want to develop a physical practice, begin simply, with a walking meditation. You don't have to go for speed or distance. Just walk with awareness. Feel each step you take; notice the scents in the air, the wind on your face, your arms moving at your sides. See the colors around you and notice sounds. When your mind wanders, bring your attention back to the feel of your steps as you walk.

If movement is limited or not possible for you, try this visualized asana practice that I led Francesco through. See yourself doing these movements in your powerful mind, knowing that your body is receiving very real benefits with each imagined motion. (If you can move, go ahead and try this modified Sun Salutation.)

1. Begin with Tadasana, Mountain Pose. See yourself standing, your feet as close together as is comfortable. Your legs are strong and straight, without locking your knees. Your tailbone is angled slightly toward the floor; your spine, the main energy channel of your body, is long. Your arms are at your sides, hands relaxed. Your chin is parallel to the floor. (Note: This pose relieves muscle tension through proper skeletal alignment.)

2. Bring your palms together in front of your chest, connecting with your breath and your heartbeat.

3. Reach out in front of you and raise your arms up overhead. Look up at your thumbs, feeling a slight arch in your upper back.

4. Bring your arms out in front of you and bend down, keeping your spine lengthened as you fold forward. It's not important to touch your toes, and you can bend in your knees here.

5. Bend your knees and bring your hands to the outsides of your feet. Take your left foot back into a lunge and bring your knee to the floor. Come to your fingertips, lift your chest, and gaze forward.

6. Take your right foot back as you press into your palms, and raise your hips up, making the shape of an upside-down V. This is Downward-Facing Dog.

7. Bring your knees to the floor and lower your hips toward your heels and your head and arms to the floor. (If your head is not on the floor, make fists and stack them one on top of the other and rest your forehead on them.) Take a deep breath and relax everything in Balasana, Child's Pose.

8. Raise your hips back up into Downward-Facing Dog. Feel how strong your arms and legs are as they support you.

9. Move your left foot up between your hands (you can give it a hand and bring it forward if it needs an assist) and let your right knee rest on the floor. Come to your fingertips to broaden your chest, and gaze forward.

10. Bring your right foot up to meet your left and fold forward. You can keep your knees bent if that feels better for you. Feel your spine long, your legs strong.

11. Bend your knees. Reach in front of you and press your feet into the floor to come up, arcing your arms up and overhead. Look up at your thumbs and feel the slight back bend beneath your shoulder blades.

12. Return to standing upright in Tadasana, Mountain Pose, with your palms together at the center of your chest.

In your Yoga Mind journal, note the feelings you had during your asana meditation (whether physical or visualized). Commit to doing your personal asana practice at least once more this week, adding another round the next time.

sun salute practice

1   2   3   4   5

6   7   8

9   10   11   12

mindful shifts

Savasana is a pause, a time in yoga classes between asana poses to rest, take a few breaths, and prepare for what comes next. Here, we pause to reflect on the work you've done so far and to take a look at the next group of yoga tools.

You'll now begin to shift into some more introspective work. The yoga tools you'll be learning to use in the next few days will help you take a look at attitudes toward yourself that you may not even be aware of. These tools are:

* **Maitri**—Kindness. We're always encouraged to be kind to others; this tool reminds us to be kind to ourselves as well. Here, it helps you develop a healthier, happier relationship with your body.

* **Satya**—The tool of compassionate honesty that allows you to turn truth into a catalyst for positive change, for both yourself and the world. You'll also

see the example of one person who, using this tool, changed the lives of millions.

* **Saucha**—A sort of spiritual spring cleaning, the yoga tool of purity lets you examine what works for you and discard what doesn't, in your home, your heart, and your head.

* **Aparigraha**—A tool that helps us get to that balanced place between fear of not having enough and taking too much, gradually finding our own personal definition of "just right." This tool helped me overcome disordered eating.

* **Asteya**—A beautiful lesson in giving, receiving, and spiritual generosity.

* **Pratyahara**—A powerful way to tune in to your own divinely given intuition.

* **Santosha**—A tool that helps us release "I'll be happy when _____" and experience contentment right now, with a special mantra and an exercise for letting go.

And now, pause. Smile. If you can, stretch your arms out wide with a lovely deep breath, and as you exhale, wrap your arms around your body and give yourself a hug.

Let's begin.

day 9

maitri

(MY-tree)
Kindness, friendliness;
the intention to bring happiness.

In *The Yoga Sutras of Patanjali*, one of the most important spiritual texts of yoga, maitri is part of what's known as the Four Locks and Keys—principles that help us navigate relationships. These locks and keys form a strategy of simple wisdom: emulate people who are happy, have compassion for those who are unhappy, be inspired by those who do good, and ignore the mean-spirited. (You can pray for them, but Patanjali's advice leans toward not wasting too much energy trying to change them.)

Of the Four Lock and Key strategies, maitri is the first: make friends with people who are sunny-side up. When you meet someone who has a positive outlook on life, learn from them by becoming a friend. Or, if they're as famous as Elizabeth Gilbert, by friending them on Facebook.

Befriending someone who is oriented toward happiness is good advice, but I wonder how much we can learn from others before we make friends with ourselves.

As you saw from the ahimsa practice on day three, our inner dialogue can be anything but kind. A steady stream of self-criticism may mask itself as plain thought, but the reality is more judgment, based on opinion. How many times have you said, aloud or to yourself, *I was so bad last night*, in reference to something you ate? That you ate something is fact; your opinion about it, and the harsh judgment of yourself, is not. It's self-criticism based on ideas we have about ourselves and the way we want things to be, which is usually different than the way they are.

In the months following the accident, Francesco's body was still going through a series of changes that had not just physical effects but emotional repercussions as well. His severed nerves were unable to deliver information from his body to his brain about temperature, so at odd times he would begin to sweat, as though the room had become blazingly hot. This made his skin break out in acne. Although this didn't seem, relatively, to be one of his bigger concerns, it still had an impact. It was yet another sign of how the accident affected everything in his life, and Fran felt he looked terrible.

He began avoiding mirrors. He chose to stay in his pajamas or hospital pants, not seeing the point of getting dressed; he didn't want to go anywhere. He instructed his family, who tended to his care, to buzz his handsome chestnut hair off, saying, "It doesn't matter what I look like anymore."

Francesco's thoughts about his body changed suddenly after a catastrophic accident. For most of us, our relationship with our physical selves changes slowly, over time—like when we notice signs of age: weight gain, creaky knees, eyes that don't work the way they used to, sagging bits. But you don't have to be aging to have a contentious relationship with your body. While working at women's magazines, I met many young women, and some men, who were harshly critical of their bodies, no matter what they looked like. I'd been much the same myself, never missing an opportunity when coming out of the shower or trying on clothes to mentally attack my own poor thighs—as if they'd ever done anything wrong.

If this sounds familiar to you, then you know how bad it feels to attack your physical self. Now imagine what it might feel like to engage in a positive relationship with your body.

Ahimsa is not causing harm to others or to ourselves. Maitri is the next step, cultivating a kind, compassionate, and ultimately loving relationship. Maitri is written about in relation to others, but what beautiful shifts might happen if we treated ourselves this way?

During Francesco's period of hiding, I told him something Swami Satchidananda had said: "We are not the body or the mind." The guru's point was that everything changes. Our bodies go from infant to child to adult to elder. Our minds can change—a person who hated radishes as a kid becomes an expert at making little rosettes of them because she can't have a salad without them. We can let go of long-standing resentments and embrace people as they are. Nothing is set or permanent, Swami Satchidananda said, except the spirit, the divine light within us all.

Francesco found this "not the body, not the mind" idea helpful. He—the essence of who he was—was eternal; always was, always would be. His body had undergone change, yes. But so could his perspective.

We began meditating on a view of his body as an entity in need of care and good stewardship. He began thinking well of his body; it was trying its best after trauma and healing itself admirably, finding its way. So were his emotions. He began to see himself as having a miraculous body and a resilient mind. Most important, he began to see the divine light within himself making all this possible.

yoga mind practice:
Making Friends with Yourself Through Maitri

Your assignment today is to practice a form of spiritual detachment, seeing your body and mind as entities in your care.

If someone gave you a puppy or a baby to care for, you would be kind to it, give it healthful food; a blanket; toys; a warm, soft bed; and love. You wouldn't criticize it or speak to it harshly, pointing out perceived flaws. So why do that to yourself?

Your emotional well-being isn't the only thing affected by negative thinking; your body is also affected by your thoughts. In 2009, the medical journal *Circulation* reported that in a research group of over 97,000 women, those who were more

Valid through 9/30/2021

Buy Any 2 Freshly Baked Cookies, Brownies, or Scones Get 1 FREE

Mix or Match Select Items

To redeem: Present this coupon in the cafe.

X3C7W8B

Items purchased as part of a Buy One Get One or Buy Two, Get Third Free offer are available for exchange only, unless all items purchased as part of the offer are returned, in which case such items are available for a refund (in 30 days). Exchanges of the items sold at no cost are available only for items of equal or lesser value than the original cost of such item.

Opened music CDs, DVDs, vinyl records, electronics, toys/games, and audio books may not be returned, and can be exchanged only for the same product and only if defective. NOOKs purchased from other retailers or sellers are returnable only to the retailer or seller from which they were purchased pursuant to such retailer's or seller's return policy. Magazines, newspapers, eBooks, digital downloads, and used books are not returnable or exchangeable. Defective NOOKs may be exchanged at the store in accordance with the applicable warranty.

Returns or exchanges will not be permitted (i) after 30 days or without receipt or (ii) for product not carried by Barnes & Noble.com, (iii) for purchases made with a check less than 7 days prior to the date of return.

Policy on receipt may appear in two sections.

Return Policy

With a sales receipt or Barnes & Noble.com packing slip, a full refund in the original form of payment will be issued from any Barnes & Noble Booksellers store for returns of new and unread books, and unopened and undamaged music CDs, DVDs, vinyl records, electronics, toys/games and audio books made within 30 days of purchase from a Barnes & Noble Booksellers store or Barnes & Noble.com with the below exceptions:

Undamaged NOOKs purchased from any Barnes & Noble Booksellers store or from Barnes & Noble.com may be returned within 14 days when accompanied with a sales receipt or with a Barnes & Noble.com packing slip or may be exchanged within 30 days with a gift receipt.

A store credit for the purchase price will be issued (i) when a gift pessimistic and cynical had greater risk of heart disease; the optimists had a lower rate. The Mayo Clinic associates positive thinking with increased life span, better coping skills during times of stress, and improved immune system response. (For more on the incredible health benefits of positive thinking, as well as ways to cultivate positivity, read the very practical and useful guide *How We Choose to Be Happy* by Rick Foster and Greg Hicks. This book is required reading in Awakening Joy, an online meditation-based happiness program that I wrote about for *The Oprah Magazine*.)

Science has proven that we can create new neural pathways in the brain—you can teach an old dog new tricks. We can do this by introducing new practices, starting with your daily three-part breathing practice.

As usual, sit or lie down comfortably. Place one hand on your heart and the other on your belly, if that's comfortable for you. Attune your attention to your breathing, and follow the instructions for Deergha Swasam from day two. After a few rounds, let your breathing find its own natural rhythm. Then introduce this mantra to your practice, repeating it silently to yourself:

I am a channel of kindness.

Repeat that mantra to yourself several times as you go through the day, particularly if you feel any negative thoughts arising.

The second part of your assignment is to treat yourself with kindness and compassion throughout the day. Use your mantra. Praise yourself for doing something well, or even at all; everyone has those "small victories" days when just making the bed is a major achievement. Do something nice for yourself that you would do for someone else, like getting a healthy snack, and thank yourself. It sounds silly, and that's fine—laughter is healthy, too. The point is that as you go through your day, treat yourself as you would treat someone you love.

At the end of the day, note your feelings in your Yoga Mind journal.

---

maitri tea

This is my version of chai, the milky, sweet Indian tea drink, minus the caffeine. It's a way of practicing kindness to your adrenal glands, which can get overtaxed by caffeine. Give them a break and brew a batch of this stress-free drink. This makes enough for at least four cups, depending on how much milk you add, and is good hot or cold. Definitely use whole spices rather than ground ones; you'll be straining this mixture, and ground spices leave sludge at the bottom. (Note: There are premade decaf chai mixes available, but I find there's way too much sugar in them. Plus making your own gives the kitchen a warm, spicy aroma.)

ingredients
6 whole cloves
3 cinnamon sticks
1 piece fresh ginger about half the size of your thumb, cut into equal-sized slices
1 tablespoon cardamom pods (usually available in the spice, Indian, Asian, or Spanish food aisle of your supermarket)

4 tea bags of decaffeinated black tea
Milk (any kind)
Honey or maple syrup

instructions

Bring five cups of water to a boil. Add the spices, reduce heat, and let mixture simmer for fifteen minutes. Turn off heat and add tea bags, letting them steep for five minutes. Sit and have a nice meditation while the tea steeps, breathing in the aroma of the spices. Strain, keeping spiced liquid and discarding solids. *Jai!* You have chai.  Add milk and natural sweetener to your preferred level of lightness and sweetness. If you like your tea extra creamy, heat the milk before adding. Don't forget to thank yourself.

day 10

satya

(SAHT-ya)
Truth;
compassionate honesty;
mindful communication.

Be a lamp to yourself. Be your own confidence.
Hold on to the truth within yourself as to the only truth.
—The Buddha

The truth shall set you free.
—John 8:32

W atch this," Francesco said.

I watched. Fran grinned as he paused theatri-
cally, like a magician about to pull off a major trick, and reached
toward me.

"Whoa!" I cried. "Did you just move your arms? Did I
see that?" Fran was nodding triumphantly. "Do it again! Do it
again!" Fran again extended his arms. They came forward only

a few inches, and there was no motion in his hands, other than going with the flow. But for someone who'd been told he would never move anything below his shoulders again, this was nothing short of magical. This meant more nerves along his spinal cord injury had somehow knit themselves together. We both hooted and hollered so loudly that Nonni came rushing in from the kitchen to see what was going on.

I was particularly grateful for this small miracle because I'd started to become worried about Francesco. Time was passing, and the most marked changes had been happening around him, not to him. Fall was painting the leaves around his house lively oranges, reds, and golds. A small area off the living room had been remodeled to create a new room, and in it were installed the hospital bed, the air-hoist lift, and a desk with a computer. Living independently had, for the foreseeable future, translated to getting a new room in his family home.

Occasionally, Fran's usual cheery optimism peeled away, exposing the raw nerves of truth. He confessed that guilt over the way his accident had affected his family weighed heavily enough to crush him. His parents worked long hours and then cared for him at home when his aide left for the day, and he felt responsible. He was sick with concern about money. There was an at-home nursing aide five days a week, the hospital bed, the wheelchair, the new wheelchair-accessible van necessary to drive him to physical therapy, physical therapy itself . . . Insurance only covered so much.

It hurt to see him so upset, but I was honored that he felt comfortable enough with me to be honest. I also knew that when the door is opened to truth, what enters is change.

Satya, the Sanskrit word for "truth," is another of the yamas, the attitudes to cultivate toward others. Those living the path of yoga are encouraged to be honest, though with compassion. Will truth violate the principle of ahimsa and cause harm? This is a big question, one we were advised in yoga teacher training to consider carefully before speaking or taking action.

As with all the ethical principles to be used in relation to others, they reflect back like mirrors, applying to us as well. How can we be honest with others if we're lying to ourselves? I understood Francesco's attempts at being cheerful around his family to keep them from worrying even more about him than they already did, but there was only so long he could keep that up. Time was ushering in the reckoning of a new truth to go with Francesco's new reality. But truth is not something to be feared. Truth, when we face it and admit it, gifts us with an opportunity to change.

Over and over, in spiritual circles and office meetings, we're encouraged to practice acceptance. This originally meant looking at reality and not losing precious time in denial or wishing things were different. "Take things as they are," people say, or "It is what it is." But acceptance shouldn't be mistaken as a cousin of apathy; these two are not blood relations. We must accept what is, yes, but by waking up to truth, we can then take action.

What you do may not necessarily be what you *want* to do. Francesco wanted more than anything to walk and regain the use of his body that he'd had before, but that wasn't going to happen immediately, if ever. This didn't mean there was nothing he could do. In fact, facing his situation spurred him into action.

After the shock of his new situation wore off, even as he went through the stages of grief associated with a traumatic event, he and his family mobilized to find out all they could about spinal cord injuries, or SCI, and what could be done. They reached out to the Christopher and Dana Reeve Foundation. They sought out researchers doing clinical trials and studies on SCI. With a mixture of charm, determination, and occasional pushiness, Fran got himself signed up for some of the studies. When the physical therapy in the hospital proved to be limited, he found more proactive physical therapy. The results, Francesco's increased movement, were a parallel victory along with acting on his own behalf.

None of this could have been accomplished if Francesco had not first looked with clear eyes and an open mind at the truth. We must practice acceptance, yes. Then we can take action. Satya—truth, and being honest with ourselves—is not an ending, but a new beginning.

yoga mind practice:
Be the Change with Satya

The great leader Mahatma Gandhi is quoted as saying, "Be the change you want to see in the world." You can create the change you want to see in your own world by using the tool of satya, or truth.

Begin with your usual Deergha Swasam practice. Do a few rounds of three-part breathing, then find your own natural breathing rhythm. You don't have to do anything specific during this practice; just by doing it regularly, you're getting into a routine of starting your day in a calming way. You're also teaching yourself how to bring about a sense of calm almost immediately, if and when stress arises during the day.

Today, as you go throughout your day, observe your feelings about your routines. Remember that observation is attention without judgment. See where your feelings become stronger. Where do you feel frustration, gratitude, relief, sadness, joy? Make quick notes in your Yoga Mind journal, but don't feel the need to take action at this time. Many harsh words have been spoken by people who defend their hurtful behavior by tacking on, "Hey, I'm just being honest." Being truthful doesn't mean being cruel, and we're working on creating positive change within ourselves, not changing other people to suit us.

Later, at home, review your list and look for truth you may have been hiding from. Are there areas of your life that you want to change? This doesn't mean you have to make sweeping alterations immediately, like quitting your job tomorrow. For now, wherever you become aware of strong feelings, look for satya, the truth of how you feel. Ask yourself these questions, writing the answers in your Yoga Mind journal:

Have you always felt this way?

Has something happened to affect the way you feel about this situation?

What are the possible benefits of this situation? (Sometimes they're hidden until you list them.)

What modifications can you make to this situation that would make it more comfortable for you? Which of your many talents and skills can be utilized to bring benefit to all concerned?

Use your yoga tool of maitri, kindness and compassion, to see the ways you might improve this area of your life or current situation, or to begin laying the groundwork for changes that won't upend your life but will enhance it. Use what satya has helped you discover to open the door to mindful change.

---

satyagraha: a guiding principle

If I told you that a nation of hundreds of millions could be freed from oppressive governmental rule by one man, you might find that hard to believe. Yet that's exactly what happened in India thanks to Mohandas K. Gandhi.

His beginnings were both humble and humbling; he came from an average family, and as an adult he was a complete failure in his career as a lawyer. His desire to steer clear of the intimidating courtroom led him to become a mediator, helping parties settle their differences through conflict resolution.

One night, Gandhi was forcibly removed from a train for sitting in a whites-only car. The next train wasn't due until morning, and Gandhi spent the long, dark night asking his soul what to do. How could he deal with his anger at a racist, oppressive government? Trying to ignore it was no longer possible, but succumbing to hatred could make him as bad as what he was fighting.

Throughout the night Gandhi weighed options, temptations, damnations. It sounds very much like the dark night the Buddha sat through under the bodhi tree until enlightenment came.

It came for Gandhi, too. He realized he could be an agent of positive change through peaceful protest, non-violence, civil disobedience, and the kind of conflict resolution he had been employing to avoid intense arguments in the courtroom. He called this guiding principle satyagraha, a combination of *satya*, the Sanskrit word for "truth" and "rightness"—what is morally and ethically just—and *graha*, which means "steadfastness." Satyagraha is the unwavering path of what is honestly right. Using satyagraha in various ways, Gandhi freed India after two hundred years of British rule.

Here in America, Dr. Martin Luther King Jr. studied Gandhi's principles of satyagraha and used the Indian leader's methods in the fight for civil rights. Satyagraha is not limited to politics and can be used as a guiding principle by all of us, at work, at home, and in our own lives.

day 11

saucha

(SOW-cha)
Cleanliness;
purity.

Yoga teacher training groups are made up of all different kinds of people. There are those you'd expect to see: people who live and breathe yoga, who are usually vegetarian or vegan, a little boho-hippie-ish, and probably own a tambourine. There are also some less expected folks: corporate types dropping out of high-stress business environments, nurses seeking to expand the ways they can help their patients, retirees, students, schoolteachers, moms crafting a career with child-friendly hours, and more. In one training program, my study partner was an Orthodox Jewish woman who wanted to bring yoga to people in her temple. Her husband thought she was engaging in some kind of idol worship until she explained yoga to him. The point is, not everyone who comes to yoga teacher training is a dyed-in-the-sustainably-sourced-wool yogi.

Yet during the many training programs I attended and co-taught, all of the students, regardless of how "yoga" they were or not, would go through some changes over the course of the program. If they ate meat, they'd start trying more vegetarian food. If they were already vegetarian, they ate even cleaner or tried a juice fast. Smokers quit smoking, and some people quit drinking. Nobody asked them to do these things, and they weren't course requirements. They were the changes that occurred very organically to people after learning about saucha, the yoga principle of cleanliness. Saucha is about purifying the body and the mind, so people started with the physical ways to do this. But those weren't the really interesting changes.

By inviting yoga into their lives, through regular asana and the study and practice of spiritual principles, the trainees began examining habits and patterns of thinking that had been on autopilot for years. "TV shows are so violent!" said a student one day. "I mean, I guess they always were, but it's like I never noticed it before. Now that I do, I don't want to watch them."

My own experience with saucha revealed that eating sweets had gone from an occasional pleasure to a daily necessity to soothe stress. That was something I'd done as a child; on the way home from school, where being bullied was a regular occurrence, I'd pick up a box of Entenmann's chocolate fudge cake. I'd carefully cut out one square piece, a normal-sized serving, and set it on a nice plate. That was for my mother. While I waited for her to come home from work, I'd methodically eat the entire rest of the cake, one bite at a time, gradually sinking into a sugar coma that calmed my nerves.

I was barely aware that this sugar-as-coping-skill had quietly flared up again and become a habit in times of stress. The principle of saucha, applied to my diet, made me see the bigger picture: my issue wasn't that I ate sugar, it was *why* I was eating it so often that I needed to look at. Saucha also helped me see the domino effect of eating so much sugar—weight gain and periods of fatigue and mild depression from sugar imbalance, which only made me more upset and had me reaching again for a sugary treat. Through saucha, I was alerted to the low-level emotional turmoil that had me returning to my childhood sugar fix. Then I could begin addressing what troubled me in healthier, more direct ways, like meditation and talking with people.

There can be a lot of black and white thinking on the spiritual path. It's not unusual to find yoga people who don't merely refuse to watch violence on TV, they don't even own a TV. Or they're not just vegetarian but vegan, and not just vegan but gluten-and-sugar-free. (By the way, I have nothing against the occasional dessert. I'm talking about unmindful consumption.) Yoga is viewed as a path to balance, but people can still go to extremes.

I learned that only after I went from one TV-watching, meat-eating, sugar-craving extreme to the other. The ironic twist was that in an effort to embrace this spiritual path of selfless service, I became self-obsessed. I was focused almost entirely on my dietary and lifestyle choices, and I asked others to bend to my restrictions when it came to eating out or what movie to see or TV show to watch. And yes, it made me a total drag.

By going to extremes, I found the true, balanced meaning of saucha: it's a spiritual spring cleaning. I started with my ideas of "bad" and "good." Most things, such as wine and sugar and TV, are benign, not inherently bad. It's the way we use these things that should be evaluated from time to time. Evaluation means weighing the *value* of something in our lives and asking if it serves us, if the relationship is harmonious.

Saucha is defined as "purity," but it's not perfectionism. It's about releasing that which no longer serves in a way that works for you, physically, emotionally, and spiritually. Saucha helps you clear the way to a purer, more authentic *you*.

yoga mind practice:
Spiritual Spring Cleaning with Saucha

You can practice saucha, or cleanliness, in any area of your life. You can use it to go through your home and take inventory of your possessions to see if they still serve you, or if it's time to release them and let them be used by someone else or recycled. You can use it as a tool for evaluating input: Does the amount of time you spend on social media enhance your life? Is TV fun, a form of stress relief, a substitute for connection? Saucha helps you examine relationships. We tend to think of relationships as being only with people, but we are actually relating to everything around us. Saucha shines a light on mutually beneficial interactions, those that are more complicated, those we can change for the better, and the ones we can release.

Simply meditating on saucha prompts consideration and starts a process of purging things that no longer work for you. Today, start your daily Deergha Swasam practice, breathing in three parts deeply and gently. After a moment or two, allow your breath to find its own natural rhythm. Then, meditate on saucha with this mantra:

I welcome what serves me and release what does not.

Keep in mind that what serves you helps you to serve others. What brings you serenity helps you to be a channel of serenity in this world. Evaluating what works for you and what doesn't is a worthwhile spiritual action. You may be surprised at what holds you back from becoming the best version of yourself.

I once took saucha to my closet, thinking I'd just purge some clothes I wasn't using. I found a few shirts and slacks from my corporate-job days. They were attractive and in fine condition, but I suddenly saw the truth of why I'd been keeping these clothes long after I'd finished my corporate office career: a fear-based thought that went, *Better hang on to them in case writing doesn't work out and you need to get a "real" job.* This thought that I hadn't been consciously aware of was sabotaging me every single day, each time I walked into my closet. I immediately donated the clothes to a charitable organization that gives disadvantaged women outfits for job interviews. Shortly after that, I finished writing the proposal for this book and found my publisher. You never know what saucha can show you.

Your saucha meditation doesn't have to be long, just a few minutes or longer, if you like. What's more important than the length of your meditation is using saucha as a lens for evaluation throughout your day. Pause when engaging in habits. Notice if something resonates in some way and silently use your mantra: *I welcome what serves me and release what does not.* Then, simply observe.

Try not to use the labels *good* and *bad*. Remember, sugar wasn't my problem, but saucha helped me look at the cause of my sugar habit and find emotional disturbance I hadn't been aware of. The act of noticing, without judgment, reduces the seductive magic of the thing or habit while empowering the observer with svadhyaya, or self-knowledge. (You'll learn more about svadhyaya in an upcoming chapter.)

Make notes of what you find in your Yoga Mind journal under two headings: "What Serves Me" and "What I Can Release." How you act upon what you find will reveal itself as you go along in the program.

---

don't find balance; find *your* balance

In order to fulfill the sense of belonging we all naturally want, we usually adopt the habits of the people around us. From school to work, as children and teenagers and then adults, we learn to fit in by going with the flow. But over time, we may see the truth: We don't live other people's lives, we don't live in other people's bodies, and what works for one person may not work for another.

When teaching yoga classes, I noticed that seasoned students would modify or sit out poses that didn't work for their bodies. These students knew themselves, and they knew there's nothing wrong with saying that something didn't feel right for them. They were still part of the class and enjoyed it all the more for not getting hurt. And usually, one person sitting out or modifying a pose helped another to say, "I'm not sure this works for me either." That allowed me to show them how to modify the pose to what was right for them.

Even though I was the teacher in these classes, these students taught me that we don't always need to do what everyone else is doing. Their beautiful lesson expanded to show me how to honor my body, and myself, in other ways. I learned to think, *These pants don't fit me*, instead of *I can't fit into these pants*. There's nothing wrong with my body, but those pants, just like that yoga pose, may not work for me.

Yoga is being in harmony. What harmony looks like for you may be different from what it looks like for someone else. Your body may thrive on a vegan diet, or it may not be able to tolerate it. If the latter is true, you can find balance by eating animal protein that is as sustainably and humanely sourced as possible. We honor our individual satya—truth—and find our own balance.

Achieving balance actually means learning how to fluctuate the way a surfer moves this way and that to stay on her board as the wave beneath her undulates, constantly changing as it moves forward—just like life. The tools of yoga teach you how to find your own balance and stay on your spiritual surfboard, no matter what.

day 12

aparigraha

(ah-pah-rih-GRA-ha)
Non-greed, non-hoarding;
taking, or accepting,
what is appropriate.

Just enough; just right. That explains aparigraha. It only partially explains why I became a smuggler.

As I entered Francesco's house and gave Nonni the European double cheek kiss, I shifted the bag I was holding behind me so that she wouldn't see it. Nonni led me to Fran's room, and as he and I greeted each other, she went off to get us some tea. "What's in the bag?" Fran asked. I put my finger to my lips with a tiny conspiratorial smile. Fran lit up at the thought of a secret surprise.

Nonni came back with the tea, asked Francesco if there was anything else he needed, and then left to go make one of her incredible home-cooked meals. Now I could get down to the serious spy business at hand. I dug into the paper shopping bag carefully, so it wouldn't make any rustling noises, and pulled out the contraband: a gold box filled with fancy chocolates.

Fran gasped. "Oh my God, you're saving my—"

"*Shhh!*" My finger snapped back up to my lips. Fran went quiet but mouthed *Hurry!* Quickly, quietly, I unwrapped the gold box and opened the lid close to him. The scent of cocoa, sweetness, and exotic flavorings wafted out, and Fran did a little aroma swoon. Then he regarded the delicate pieces in the box as if he were a jewel thief surveying a velvet tray of precious gems. "Truffles," he whispered. "Dark chocolate cherry filled, vanilla caramels . . . Wait, what's that one? Never mind, just give it to me."

I popped the mystery candy into his mouth. "What was it?"

His expression was dreamy as he slowly chewed. "I don't know," he said, "but it was amazing. Another, please."

He was savoring the third chocolate, and I was *mmmm*-ing over one, too, when Nonni came back in. We were now smugglers caught red-handed, or in this case, cocoa-fingered. Bless Nonni's heart, she knew what was going on but played innocent. "More tea?" she asked. Our mouths full, we just shook our heads.

The Great Chocolate Caper was a secret mission because of something Francesco had mentioned in passing the week before. A family friend had sent a box of chocolates to the house as a holiday gift, but after a few, Fran was cut off. "You're getting heavy," his sister, Charlotte, told him. "I'm having trouble pushing your wheelchair up the ramp. We have to watch your weight." With no way for Fran to exercise, and his mother and sister both strong but petite, slender wheelchair pilots, calories had to be counted. Fran had related this to me as a funny story, but it stuck with me long after the telling. It was bad enough that he was no longer able to physically take a chocolate out of a box for himself if he wanted one, but now even small pleasures had to be monitored.

Nothing in his life was private anymore. Showering, getting dressed, eating, and even bathroom business were all assisted by a family member or nursing aide. I thought there should be at least one thing he could have a say over, and my solution was a small box of chocolates that was his and his alone, for him to say how many he wanted.

I didn't see much harm in giving Fran the forbidden chocolates because I knew from the way he and his family ate and conducted themselves that he wouldn't overdo it. Just as I'd thought, he savored three and then said, "Okay, I'm good." Fran and his family were a tribe naturally attuned to aparigraha, or non-greed.

In yoga teacher training, I'd learned that the prefix *a-* forms the opposite of a word. *Pari* means "on all sides" and *graha*, "to grab." So, *parigraha* means taking too much, whenever and however possible; *aparigraha* means the opposite, only taking what is needed.

As I mentioned in the previous chapter, I knew something about this. Maybe because food is something children can get their hands on with relative ease, my way of working through fear became, from a very early age, eating. And there were a fair amount of things to be anxious about when I was a child. I was loved and well cared for, but my quiet, bookish nature; lack of athleticism; and huge glasses made me a target for bullies at school. My nana's dying suddenly when I was seven had a severe impact on me. My divorced mom and I lived in a neighborhood that bordered a lively middle-class shopping and residential area and a part of town most people avoided. A couple of blocks down one way and there was excellent cherry pie to be had; a couple of blocks uptown and we kids were told to be on the lookout for a friend's schizophrenic father, who had last been seen wandering around the school with a Bible and a hunting knife.

As a child, I ate off my fear. As an adult, I unconsciously fine-tuned the anxious-eating impulse and upped the game with controlled eating. I tried a variety of diets, such as fat free, vegetarian, vegan, low carb, low calorie, high carb, high protein, and others. I reframed my eating issues as lifestyle regimens. Being vegetarian and vegan made me feel highly ethical (and I became very righteous about that, until I lost the energy to feel or do much of anything). Or, when I tried another regimen, it meant that I was taking extra-good care of myself. What I was really doing was trying to create a sense of control in a life that frequently felt out of my hands. The consequence was feeling even less in control. Because my true physical needs were my last concern, I ended up eating more, usually a lot more than I wanted or needed.

Overeating is one manifestation of unaddressed (but over-dressed) anxiety. A fellow student in teacher training shared a story about a girlfriend who was a hoarder. She overbought groceries and ended up having to throw a lot of food away when it rotted, unused. She kept the boxes from all her purchases, stacking them one on top of another, in case she needed them—for what, she couldn't say. She held on to clothes that should have been given away long ago. If she liked an item, she bought six in different colors, and because she did this so often, she had enough clothes and shoes still in packages and with tags on to open her own store. She didn't, though. She just kept buying until her apartment was filled, in some spaces to the ceiling, and her credit cards were maxed out. Then, frightened by her own circumstances, she'd do the thing that had previously given her temporary relief from fear: she'd shop, this time for plastic boxes to "organize" and store all the stuff in.

Another student related the story of a friend who said his husband was constantly on Facebook, scrolling down the news feed on his phone at dinner, when they were both sitting at home watching a movie. When the student brought it up, after some digging, the husband admitted he was anxious about work and was distracting himself with cute cat videos and other people's lives.

It took some time for me to see the correlation between my overeating and stress. Initially I thought the problem was food itself, that I was addicted to sugar or eating too much meat or too many carbs, and that would set me on another drastic eating plan. But no matter what I was or wasn't eating, I did notice that I ate less when I was calm.

Not long before smuggling the chocolates to Francesco, I'd been feeling anxious about a new consulting job that I was starting soon. Even though I'd been chosen by the editor in chief of this new magazine and he'd expressed a lot of confidence in my skills, I was nervous about my performance, meeting all the new people, and how I'd fit in yoga and working with Francesco.

This time, though, I had the tool of meditation. After learning about aparigraha, I gently focused on that, and I was able to see my pattern of stress–freak out–eat. Deergha Swasam helped me calm down so that I could eat more mindfully and try other things like taking a brief walk around the block instead of nervously noshing. I started eating a bit less, and interestingly, enjoying it more.

Francesco savored his forbidden chocolates. After a few days, he did tell his sister about them—mostly so she could give him one or two, but also so that he could share them with her.

yoga mind practice:
Finding What You Truly Need with Aparigraha

We are the wealthiest nation in the world, with few shortages, and a nation of overconsumption. Barely a day goes by without a news item about increases in obesity and addiction. We see more reality shows about hoarders, people who compulsively acquire food and material goods and even animals to the point of harming themselves and others. And the people suffering are not to be blamed. This is a manifestation of dis-ease that can happen to anyone.

We don't need to qualify for a reality show for overdoing to be an issue in our own lives. If somewhere within you a voice whispers, *More*, and can't seem to be sated, the yoga tool of aparigraha can help.

Aparigraha is not about restriction or dieting or cutting yourself off from things that are pleasurable and necessary. Aparigraha is like a pair of reading glasses that lets you see something more clearly, helping you become aware of behavior out of proportion to what feels manageable. As I mentioned, I thought that food was my problem, and I went on a variety of different diets and eating plans that always failed. Only after asking myself *why* I was overeating did I see the underlying anxiety that manifested in overeating and overdieting.

Aparigraha lights the path from "too much" to "just right." It is most helpful when combined with maitri, compassionate kindness. Today, try an aparigraha meditation:

1. Sit comfortably in a chair with your hands relaxed, either folded in your lap or resting faceup on your thighs. When comfortable, begin your three-part yoga breathing practice for a moment or two. Then let your breathing be wherever it wants to be. Watch the flowing waves of your inhalations and exhalations.

2. With compassion, ask yourself if there is a part of your life that often feels like a preoccupation. Eating is a common example, but there are others. You may be aware of a behavior that feels out of control, or people close to you may have tried to talk to you about something that is causing you harm. What you're looking for is something that gets a disproportionate amount of

your attention, which then has an adverse effect on the rest of your life, something where too much of one thing results in a sense of lack of another. Use the tool of maitri, being compassionate toward yourself and others; you are simply doing some investigation at this time.

3. If you find something like this, gently feel around and underneath the activity, as though turning over a stone, for emotions that accompany it. What leads you to the behavior? Again, compassion is your constant companion on this journey. Be kind to yourself as you investigate.

4. When you are satisfied that you have some answers, return to a few rounds of Deergha Swasam breathing. Then slowly open your eyes. Write what you found during your aparigraha meditation in your Yoga Mind journal with an extra helping of compassion for yourself. There are yoga tools in this book that will help you take appropriate actions. For now, simply note the behavior, and be proud of yourself for your kind and honest investigation.

Note: If you think you may have an addiction, please see the appendix at the back of this book for helpful resources.

day 13

asteya

(ASH-tay-ah)
Not stealing;
resisting the desire to take
something that doesn't
belong to us.

When I was studying to be a yoga teacher, I learned about another of the yamas, or ethical principles to practice in relationship to others: asteya, or non-stealing. The definition explained it all—stealing is wrong. Of course, this wasn't unique to yoga. We'd all heard this before in the guidelines of various religions, and from our parents, who taught us not to become baby shoplifters.

When I started training yoga teachers, I learned about other, more subtle kinds of theft. These robberies were unintentional and unconscious, and I knew this because I saw it clearly enough with students. But I couldn't see my own stealing until it was pointed out to me.

H. was a teacher in training, and she quickly stood out from the rest of the group by being habitually late. Typically, the trainees take the first week to get used to the time they need to commute from home to the yoga studio, to change into yoga clothes, and to dash downstairs to the health food store for a pre-class breakfast smoothie. They're told to get to class at least fifteen minutes ahead of start time.

From that point on, it seemed like H. had understood she should arrive at least fifteen minutes *after* start time. In a regular classroom, a late student just comes into the room and sits at a desk; it's not too disruptive. In yoga teacher training classes, students lay yoga mats out either facing one another in two rows or in a big semicircle if there's a lecture. All their stuff—backpacks, coats, textbooks, laptops, smoothies—is behind them and around them. If someone comes in late, at least half the class has to get up and start moving mats, clothes, books, and *oops*, there goes the smoothie, and now someone is dashing out for paper towels. The late person has to get a mat and props, all the while explaining that the train was late or she'd forgotten her textbook, her anxiousness changing the atmosphere of the room. The physical process of making space for her could take over five minutes, and it would take a few minutes more for everyone to settle down and focus again, and for the teacher to locate her lost train of thought.

After this happened several times, and H. became more apologetic and upset by her own lateness, the lead trainer, Rashmi (whose name means "radiant light") gave a brief lecture about asteya. "Lateness is a form of stealing," she said, gently but firmly. "We know trains can be off schedule and things can happen. But when we're consistently late, for everything, we're taking time away from whatever we're supposed to be doing or whomever we're meeting. Lateness also steals from you—it takes away your serenity and your ability to enjoy things, because you're all stressed out." Rashmi advised that if we were consistently late, we should look within to find out what was behind that.

I generally had a habit of being late—for things that I didn't want to do, like dental appointments and jobs run by tense, angry bosses. I usually had no problem being on time for, say, movies or things that I wanted to do. Now I could see that I was stealing time from others, as well as robbing myself of serenity by stressing out over the lateness and creating difficulties in other people's schedules.

The other lesson about asteya came from J., a student whose class participation was off the charts. Teachers never made it more than a quarter of the way through whatever they were presenting before her hand shot up. "Oh! Can I say something?" she'd start, not waiting for permission before talking at length about a detail from her personal practice, or something she'd read or heard about from another yoga teacher. We wanted the students to share, and we'd told them that we would leave plenty of time for their comments and questions after our presentations were done. J. would smile and nod in agreement, and then raise her hand again and again so quickly and enthusiastically I thought she'd tear a rotator cuff.

I could also relate to this behavior. As a trainer, I was eager to share my teaching experiences with the students. They seemed to be getting a lot out of it, but the senior trainers gently told me I was talking too much. This led me to think more carefully before I spoke, and to be conscious about the content of my speech. As a result, I talked less but said more.

By understanding these subtle forms of stealing, H. discovered that she was very nervous about teaching and was unconsciously avoiding coming to class. J. saw that her habit of interrupting was rooted in her coming from a large, boisterous family, where she and her siblings vied good-naturedly for their parents' attention. By using asteya as a guiding principle to forge more conscious behaviors, both H. and J. experienced freedom from the present-day effects of past difficulties, seemingly just by seeing the satya, or truth, behind their actions.

H. conquered her lateness problem by addressing her nervousness, and for the rest of the course she came to class way before start time, quietly hitting the books and practicing. She was calmer and more focused, and she passed her final exam. J., well, she still had a lot to say, but she'd raise her hand and then catch herself with, "Never mind! I'll wait." And she would, until everyone else had shared.

Practicing asteya led both students to address issues that had been holding them back and creating problems. The freedom and lightness they felt was easy to see. By doing this, they were able to practice spiritual generosity, being more considerate, thoughtful, and respectful. People responded to this and naturally gravitated toward them. Paradoxically and beautifully, by giving, they received so much more than they ever could have taken.

yoga mind practice:
Give and Receive with Asteya

Is it possible to steal from yourself? Yes, but it's hard to see. Your practice today is to do some detective work, looking for ways you may be robbing yourself of serenity. Some clues: Chronic lateness. Forgetting or losing things. Staying up late every night to watch TV even though you know you'll be bone tired the next day. Not practicing basic self-care, like making sure there's food in the house or that you engage in some exercise. (Remember the chapter on asana from day eight? Find a form of movement you look forward to doing.)

As with H., J., and myself, simply understanding that these behaviors are a form of theft can be enough to enlighten you to their true causes. Once you see that it's not really about the commute time or misplacing your keys, use asteya not merely to halt the behavior, but to go in the opposite direction, practicing spiritual generosity *toward yourself.* Your maitri practices taught you to think of yourself as the steward of your body and to care for it as you would a precious child or pet. Well, you wouldn't want that beloved being to become sick with stress, and *you* are that precious being. Give yourself the gifts of enough sleep whenever you can; of healthy food; of a walk. Set out everything you need for the next day the night before, so all is ready for you and your wonderful, miraculous body isn't flooding itself with stress hormones but rather has the parasympathetic nervous system's

Peace Response in gear. Be kind and give to yourself. What you receive will be far greater and more valuable than what you were taking before.

Begin your three-part yoga breathing practice, and when your breathing returns to its natural pace, for a few moments, silently repeat this mantra: *In giving, I receive.*

pratyahara

(PRAHT-ya-hara)
Quiet time for your senses.

Turn off our *cell phones*?"

The teacher trainees looked at us as though we'd just asked them to turn off their lungs. Trying to hold their breath might have been easier for some of the younger ones, who lived by their phones.

Rashmi and I explained the reasons for this seemingly outrageous request. "You're on a spiritual retreat that's part of your training. You're going to be teaching people about meditation—about focusing their awareness on one thing, like their breathing. In order to teach that, you have to have some experience with it." At this point, the teacher trainees began nodding—grudgingly, but they were starting to see the light. "The whole point of yoga is to bring your awareness within, remember?"

we asked. "Kind of difficult to focus and train your awareness within if you're constantly checking your text messages and posting photos online. Plus the ringing and the buzzing is distracting; you all know how much it bothers you if that happens when you're in deep relaxation in a class, right?"

More nodding, a few murmurs of agreement.

"So, yes, unless you have an emergency going on at home that you need to monitor, we're asking you to turn off your phones."

Various beeps and other electronic signals sounded as the mechanical extensions of their lives were turned off. We nodded at each other and them, glad they were willing to practice non-attachment and take this journey to a wondrous, exciting world—not just the quiet ashram in the countryside where we'd gone for our retreat, but the world within themselves.

As we walked to the meditation hall, over loamy ground and under a bright blue sky and tall trees that some of the trainees were just noticing for the first time, a voice piped up from the back of the line: "What if we just put our phones on silent?"

Ten years before that, when I had gone on retreat as a yoga teacher trainee, my instructors didn't need to have this conversation with us because none of us had a cell phone. Back then, mobile phones were the size of a brick and had to be attached to a car to work. My main concern on that retreat was how I was going to wake up in time for the mandatory six a.m. meditation session; there was no alarm clock in my dorm-style room, and I'd forgotten to bring one. "Don't worry," one of my instructors told me. "There's an ashram-style alarm clock."

The next morning, the sound of "Somewhere over the Rainbow" being played on a violin floated through the hallways. For a moment I thought the ashram's clever caretakers had installed a sound system throughout the halls. Then the sound slowly came closer. I eased out of bed and opened the door. Down the hall, walking carefully in the dim light, was a petite elder sannyasi, or nun, dressed in orange robes and playing a violin. She smiled at me, her blue eyes saying good morning under a fringe of white bangs. She continued playing as she moved on to the next floor. This was the ashram's alarm clock: Swami Gurucharanananda, also lovingly called Mataji ("Respected Mother"). *If everyone could wake up this way*, I thought, *we'd have world peace in our lifetime.*

Aside from the violin wake-up call, our mornings at the ashram were quiet, partly because we were nestled deep in the Virginia mountains, and partly by design. Our training group and the ashram residents would begin to observe silence from about nine in the evening until after breakfast the next day. After waking in the morning, we walked across a field, the rising sun illuminating dewdrops on the grass, to the meditation hall. The large carpeted room was lit just enough to find a cushion or a chair. There was nothing to look at, no need to speak, and only the sound of the birds singing outside to hear. Less input made meditating on our breathing easy.

Later, the quality of all our usual daily activities was enhanced by that period of sense withdrawal. People seemed to consider their words more carefully when they spoke, and others listened with more attention. We paused to appreciate the aromas of our breakfast tea and toast, the warmth and sweetness of our oatmeal, the tang of fruit and the richness of the nut butters. Having had the time and space to notice nothing made us notice and enjoy everything. I found myself appreciating things that normally would've passed me by.

This quiet time for the senses is a modification of the yoga tool called pratyahara, which means "sense withdrawal." In a traditional practice, it's a form of meditation where you close your eyes, sit in as quiet a place as possible with lights dimmed, and even put your hands over your ears. The idea is to give your senses a rest from input so you can experience peace, and find the peace within yourself.

It's not that easy to find such a quiet place, or the time to sit in one if we do. But we can reduce the amount of sensory input we usually take in. Today, we're exposed to more information than at any other time in history—screens are everywhere, from our pockets to almost every room in our homes, in elevators and the doctor's office, in our cars and in taxis and on mass transit. It's almost impossible not to take in advertisements and other input, unless you make a conscious decision to let your senses rest and recharge.

What are the benefits? Improved ability to focus, reduction of potential burnout due to overstimulation of the brain, and enhanced appreciation for everything around you.

On that first retreat, I remember being able to experience, and really enjoy, everything around me. I connected with people. I connected with the food I ate, and it was so satisfying. Nature—wow! I was able to learn several kinds of meditation—breathing meditation, walking meditation, repetition of mantra, even writing meditation—and really experience their benefits, because I wasn't distracted. Thanks to even brief periods of sense withdrawal, my arrival time in the present moment was much faster than when I tried to dive from *doing* to *being*.

On the retreat where I was a co-trainer, it didn't take long for the student teachers to see the benefit of a little pratyahara now and then. Just as brahmacharya helped them conserve and harness their energy, withdrawing from the constant pull of the phone and all its fun distractions, and even from talking, let them enjoy a sense of peace. Instead of aggravating their "text neck" aches—yes, that's actually a thing—they turned their faces up to feel the warmth of the sun. They enjoyed some quiet time.

And that's all it takes, just a little time for the senses to rest and be restored. After a period of what feels like nothing, we can notice and enjoy the vibrant experience of everything.

yoga mind practice:
Quiet Time with Pratyahara

The idea of withdrawing your senses—closing off your sight and hearing, not speaking, remaining still—might seem a little boring; you're not really doing anything. And that's the point. By not doing, we notice more. We experience subtleties, and we can change our relationship with the world around us.

Your pratyahara assignment today is simple: gradually withdraw your senses. Either during your regular yoga breathing practice or at a separate time, take a comfortable seat. You can also lie down. (You may fall asleep, so set a timer for ten minutes.)

First, make sure the room is quiet; silence your phone for all calls, texts, and alerts. This allows your sense of hearing to relax.

Next, feel yourself settling into your physical position; if sitting, make sure your spine is lengthened without being stiff. Place your hands on your lap or knees, wherever they're comfortable. If lying down, let your arms rest at your sides. Know that for this period of time, you don't have to move or do anything.

Now close your eyes. Let your eyes rest. Let your eyelids release, knowing there's nothing you need to see at this time.

Do a few rounds of three-part breathing, and then let your breathing find its natural rhythm. Allow yourself to enjoy the stillness around you and within you.

Your timer will wake your sense of hearing. Open your eyes slowly, and move mindfully to shut the timer off. Let your senses gradually return to their waking, active state. Record how this practice felt in your Yoga Mind journal.

day 15

santosha

(san-TOE-sha)
Contentment.

When I learned about santosha, yoga's version of contentment, it seemed right up there with enlightenment in terms of what I could accomplish in this lifetime. Cultivate a sense of being all right with who I was and what I had? Impossible. To me, contentment was fleeting and based on whether I'd gotten what I wanted, usually from some outside source. But santosha proposed a contentment that could be intentionally cultivated, independent of the external sources of happiness and value we usually count on and measure ourselves by. Santosha is being okay with what we have and who we are, right now.

Before my fellow teacher trainees and I went ballistic with hypothetical examples of why santosha was the craziest idea ever, our teachers explained that santosha wasn't some stilted form of acceptance that meant giving up on dreams or goals, or accepting painful circumstances. It certainly didn't mean someone like Francesco should do nothing to improve his condition, and with a smile on his face, no less. What santosha proposed was being okay now while going for those goals, rather than wasting priceless days, even a lifetime, thinking, *I'll be happy when . . .*

How could this be accomplished? By recognizing that our true selves are pure and perfect. Santosha offered us the opportunity to see that the time to start thinking you are whole and good and enough is now. This very moment.

Unfortunately, circumstances and perspectives make us forget that.

In fall of 2002, about six months after Francesco's accident, my friend Marnie found out why she'd been having trouble eating—food seemed to lodge in her chest and cause severe pain, like the night we went out for her birthday dinner, but worse and worse. She saw her doctor, then more doctors, and finally specialists, who found the last thing that they were expecting: a tumor the size of a golf ball in her esophagus, formed from a type of cancer that has a fatality rate of 95 percent. She was told she probably had a year or less to live.

After I got Marnie's call, I struggled to hold on to the phrase *Everything is going to be okay.* In a lucid moment as I sat sobbing on my yoga mat, where I went to try to breathe and calm down from mounting hysterics, I couldn't recall ever hearing my yoga teachers saying "Everything is going to be okay." They didn't make such general, palliative statements because they were attuned to satya, to honesty and the truth that some things in life are really not okay. And what about santosha, contentment? Just as I'd thought: impossible.

Over the next few weeks I rearranged my work schedule around Marnie's doctor visits, taking turns with her husband and best friends, each of us asking questions and taking notes. We galvanized our initial shock into determination—we would beat this thing, together! We mobilized, we researched, we planned, and perhaps most important, we used one of the best weapons against fear: humor. Marnie loved to laugh, and we dove for any opportunity to make her smile through this terrifying time.

I went with her for one of the check-in appointments before the surgery to remove her tumor. This was a series of interviews with nurses, attending physicians, and the surgeons themselves. Each came in separately and each asked the same questions, over and over and over. They did this to make sure everyone was on the same page, but around the fourth or fifth time it became a bit much for Marnie. She hadn't been able to eat anything solid in over a month and was getting by, barely, on broth and other liquids. Even those rarely stayed down. She looked adrift in a paper hospital gown.

"Name?" asked the latest physician.

"Marnie M——," she answered, her eyes vacant.

"Age?"

"Thirty-four."

"Occupation?"

Marnie sighed at the thought of having to answer *publicist* for the umpteenth time that morning, so I jumped in. "Nuclear power plant worker."

The attendant looked at the previous notes. "Uh, I'm sorry, but—"

Marnie suppressed a smile. "That's right," she said. "Toxic waste disposal division."

"That, er, isn't what I have on the notes . . . ?"

"You know, Marn, I really wish you would've worn the protective gear they gave you," I said, frowning.

She rolled her eyes. "I know, but those hazmat suits are just so baggy and unfashionable. If only they came belted. And in colors."

We were still giggling when the doctor who would perform the surgery that we hoped would turn this into a really good bad story came in. The surgeon immediately understood what was going on and smiled. Marnie and I settled down and answered his questions correctly, like good girls, but occasionally a glance at each other would make us snort-laugh again. In an oncologist's office, hearing a lot of scary statistics and no guarantees, we'd found our way back to ourselves again. We'd found a pocket of santosha.

These vehicles that our souls drive around in, our bodies, do their jobs so well and so automatically, day after day after all the days that make up a life, we're mostly unaware of just how miraculous they are.

These vehicles will break down, in different ways. Our bodies get sick, get older, and change. But yoga teaches us that the spirit is eternal. The divine light within is bright and perfect.

Knowing this, even thinking about the possibility, can help us experience santosha. It can restore a sense of peace within. This helps to generate peace all around us. For me, this was one of the keystone teachings of yoga: not everything in life is going to be okay, but *you* can be okay. Even as the storm swirls around you, you can be the calm at the center of it. It is possible to want everything in your life to be different—if your body is ill, if there's something wrong with work or a relationship, or if any of the many things we know can rock us to the core happens—and still find the natural peace within you. Knowing that you have that center within you, that perfect and brightly burning divine light that cannot be extinguished by any of life's winds, is santosha.

A variation on santosha is making peace with something that is not within your control. When Marnie received her diagnosis, the first thing I thought of, probably because of working with Francesco, was to bring yoga's tools to her—to meditate with her, do Therapeutic Yoga with her, see if yoga could somehow help her, physically and emotionally.

She didn't want this. She appreciated my offer, but given her projected life expectancy—less than a year—she wanted to take advantage of everything Western medicine had to offer. She wanted to get second opinions, find the best doctors. She also wanted to regain a sense of normalcy by going back to work in between chemo and radiation appointments. All of this was understandable, and knowing her as I did, not surprising. Marnie wasn't the meditating type.

As much of a believer in yoga as I was, I made peace with Marnie's way of dealing with her illness, and fast; I wanted to be as supportive as possible. I reminded myself that I don't live other people's lives. We don't know how we'll react in a given situation until we're in it. Each of us makes our own choices, and it's up to the people around those who have to make these choices to love and support them as much as they possibly can. That was the yoga I could give my friend. That was what she wanted from me, and santosha helped me get there.

Contentment is not an accident or a result of an external source. Santosha is a choice. When we want to be all right with who we are and what we have while working toward goals to better care for our lives and these vehicles for our souls, santosha is a compass pointing the way. It will always point within; its true north is you.

yoga mind practice:
Santosha Now

Your assignment for today: let go.

In Integral Yoga classes, we instruct a pose called Paschimottanasana, a seated forward bend in two parts. First, you reach toward your feet. Students often strain in this part, pulling themselves forward with all their might. If they can reach their toes, they pull on those poor little digits as though that's going to make their hamstrings cooperate and let them go further forward. It doesn't work.

The second part of the pose is letting go. We instruct them to let go of their feet and legs and relax their arms. Relax the shoulders. Relax the head and neck. The students are reluctant at first, but then they're relieved. They relax, sigh, close their eyes. And a funny thing starts to happen: they move further into the pose than when they were trying so hard.

Santosha is the same. We're striving so hard for things that will make us feel happy, but by letting go, we can feel contentment now. Again, this doesn't mean giving up. We all have things in life that we want or need, some of them serious. But constantly striving is exhausting and causes us to lose sight of where we are now.

For today, let go. Begin with your morning Deergha Swasam three-part breathing practice and incorporate this mantra: *Grateful for what I am, grateful for what I have.*

Repeat it silently to yourself, and incorporate it into your breathing: *Grateful for what I am* as you inhale, *grateful for what I have* as you exhale.

For today, let go of whatever you are striving for, whether it's working so hard to lose weight, getting that promotion, finding the perfect house or partner, or your expectations about others or yourself. Whatever you can let go of that won't harm you or someone else, let it go. See how it feels to release that constant effort. Repeat your Deergha Swasam practice with the mantra at midday, and again before you go to sleep.

mantra meditation:
your body is a holy temple

Having worked at women's magazines for most of my career, as well as at a few men's magazines, I can generalize and say that a lot of people are really upset with their bodies. Their anger and frustration and obsessive desire for their physical self to be different is based on perception, meaning they think theirs isn't right in some way, or circumstances, meaning they may be going through an illness that creates a sense of betrayal: "My body is turning on me."

Science has proven that our thoughts affect our bodies. Even without that proof, we have to consider the harm it does to our minds as well as our bodies to think that we're somehow "less than."

Just as pulling on your toes won't help your legs relax and stretch, negative thoughts about our bodies rarely lead to positive change. If there is something in your life that needs to be addressed, change usually comes as the result of some kind of wake-up call. But consistent negativity only causes depression and possibly even disease.

Your body is a holy temple. This is what I heard in yoga classes, and it's what I began saying to myself whenever I frowned at my dimpled thighs or found some other perceived flaw, and when my knee gave out and I hobbled around in a leg brace on crutches for a month. Whenever you catch yourself thinking negatively of your body, use that mantra: *Your body is a holy temple*—even, and especially, when your body isn't working perfectly. *Your body is a holy temple.* Say it often enough, and you will begin to remember that it's true.

finding your balance

Coming to the halfway point of a yoga class can energize some people—*Wow, look at all I've done!*—and cause others to heave a sigh and start thinking more about the part where they get to relax. This is why we take a Savasana break and pause, and why I'll say: Well done, you're halfway through! You've accomplished so much. Please give yourself a pat on the back.

In yoga classes, during this restorative break, I tell the students what's coming next. Here is a look at the next group of yoga tools you'll be learning to use:

* **Sutra 1.14**—A powerful tool that will give you the inner strength to keep going toward your sankalpa.

* **Pratipaksha Bhavana**—Also known as the Yoga Thought-Swap Trick, this handy yoga tool will help you deal with the harmful effects of negative, often false perceptions and find your true self. This

is especially helpful for situations that put you in a fearful state.

✻ **Japa**—An ancient form of meditation using mantra, its efficacy is backed up by modern neuroscience. People who think they have trouble with meditation may find it easier with this technique.

✻ **Samskaras**—A different way to look at repeating cycles of behavior that can free you from harmful habits at last.

✻ **Dhyana**—A tool that will change your relationship to meditation and make it more accessible than ever.

✻ **Titiksha**—A beautiful lesson in learning to see your own strength, especially at times when you feel your weakest. A tool that can carry you through challenging times.

✻ **Tapas**—This tool shows you how to transform painful experiences into beneficial lessons that help you grow and become the person you want to be.

✻ **Svadhyaya**—How to move away from allowing circumstances and information from outside sources to define you, and instead learn to see your true self.

With what these tools can offer giving us the energy to continue, let's take the next step.

sutra

1.14

(SOO-trah)

Don't give up on yourself.

Never give in, never give in, never, never, never, never—in nothing, great or small, large or petty—never give in except to convictions of honor and good sense.

—Sir Winston Churchill

The *Yoga Sutras of Patanjali*, one of the key philosophical texts of yoga, is composed of a series of pithy bits of wisdom known as sutras. The sutras describe experiences, ideas, and goals that help form a path to our best selves.

Although the text is nearly two thousand years old, the advice is eternally relevant. There are 196 sutras, but one is cited more than any of the others: Sutra 1.14, which reads, *Practice becomes firmly grounded when well attended to for a long time, without break, and in all earnestness.*

In other words, never give up.

Sutra 1.14 is usually interpreted to mean we should continually practice the principles of yoga so that they become second nature and the results are more tangible. My teachers broadened the meaning to include life goals beyond yoga, knowing that setbacks could lead to discouragement and quitting. And when we give up on anything, what are we really giving up on but ourselves?

"I'm going to China," Francesco announced one afternoon.

I was glad I was about to sit down when he said this because I might have fallen where I stood. Francesco's saying he was going to China was a nearly fantastical statement, given his physical condition and the changes that had brought to his life. It took great effort, coordinated by a team of people, to get him even half a mile into town. Each morning, after his daily physical needs were attended to, he was hoisted out of his hospital bed and into his wheelchair and taken to be showered. Then he was lifted back into the chair, taken back to his bed, and dressed. He'd be given his medications and fed, and then it was back to the wheelchair to be taken to the van. There, he'd be battened down in the back and driven wherever he needed to go. Just getting out the door could take two hours or more. Meeting at a restaurant in town—something Fran had recently started trying, knowing he needed to leave the house every now and then or he'd go crazy—was a big production. Now he was talking about going halfway around the world.

"China!" I said, still trying to imagine the plane trip alone. "Why? What's in China?"

Francesco explained that he'd been accepted into a new study involving surgical implantation of stem cells in the spine. There was anecdotal evidence of people with ALS, or Lou Gehrig's disease, and multiple sclerosis experiencing improvement, sometimes dramatic. Francesco wanted to try the procedure to see if it would have any effect on his spinal cord injury, possibly regenerating nerves.

As is typical with studies and experimental treatments, there were no guarantees, but this time there were many issues. Fran would have to bring all his own post-surgery medical supplies, such as catheter kits; the Chinese hospital didn't provide them. He'd be in Beijing for a month—a few weeks before surgery, then after, for recuperation time. He'd need family members there to care for him, because much of the post-surgery time would be out of the hospital, in a nearby hotel. And then there was the eighteen-hour trip, not including the time to get to the airport and then to the hospital. We didn't even go into how much it would cost; obviously, insurance wasn't going to cover any of this. To top it all off, the surgery might have no effect. And of course Francesco was ready to face it all. He had already made up his mind to go.

His only hesitation was about his mother and sister, who would have to take time off from work and medical school to go with him. Not surprisingly, they hadn't given that a moment's thought before saying yes.

Francesco related all of this with grounded realism. He understood the arduousness of the trip and the risks of the surgery. He didn't talk about being able to walk again. He said,

"There's a chance it could help. And if there's even the slightest chance of any kind of improvement, I'll try it, whatever it is." There was only one thing that he could say with certainty: "I have to keep going."

Doctors had told Francesco to move on, meaning to accept his new status as a quadriplegic in a wheelchair. Fran had decided not to "move on," whatever that meant, but to keep going. I would call him brave, but he would say that he was not as courageous as he was terrified about the idea of giving up.

He also knew that focusing on a specific goal, like walking, could trigger frustration if that didn't come to pass, which could infect him with apathy. He couldn't afford that. He kept to the core of his mantra, getting better. And in order to get better he had to keep going. Without break, in all earnestness, just as Sutra 1.14 says we must, if we are to accomplish anything.

Francesco had no idea what would happen when he made this long and difficult journey and had this intensive surgery, but trying meant he'd already traveled much further than China. Just by trying, he was getting better.

yoga mind practice:
Keep Going with Sutra 1.14

You are halfway along your Yoga Mind journey. As I'm writing this, I'm thinking of you and congratulating you for what you've accomplished so far. I'm smiling at you, because we're fellow travelers on this path.

Your practice today is to look back at the sankalpa you set at the beginning. Look at what you wrote in your Yoga Mind journal about your intention. Is your goal the same? Has it changed in some way? Do you know now that the goal is only part of this journey?

The real point is that you can now see what you are capable of. It doesn't matter if you've done the program so far in a perfectly imperfect way; you've gotten to this point because you kept going. Some difficulties may have come up. Maybe you've seen some things along the way that you weren't expecting, possibly even weren't thrilled about. You kept going. That is what we do, and what we must do. Always.

And now, you are here. Pause for a moment as you would at a place with an excellent view. Take a selfie, if you like, and print it out and put it in your Yoga Mind journal. (And post it in the Spiritual Surfer Sangha group on Facebook at https://www.facebook.com/SpiritualSurferSangha/!) Give yourself a hearty *Jai!* ("Victory!") Congratulate yourself for the work you have done so far, as I am congratulating you.

We are all together on this path. Our goals may be different, but we are a sangha, traveling together, sharing strength. How beautiful. How beautiful and strong you are.

Never give up on yourself. Know that you may have to give up on other things—sometimes we have to leave jobs or relationships, or let go of ideas we had about ourselves, such as thinking we can't change. Those are things that can be released. But you keep going. Whatever you need to try that can help you to see that divine light burning within you, try it. Keep going.

Visit the Spiritual Surfer Sangha on Facebook and let the group know you're at the halfway point so we can cheer you on with a heartfelt *jai!*

the ego: hero or villain?

Is the ego bad? Or does it just have a bad rap? The answer depends on whether you cleave more to Western or Eastern thought.

The word *ego* is Latin for "I," and in America and other Western nations, we know the word from its use by Sigmund Freud, father of psychoanalysis, and others in his field to denote a core sense of self. It's what makes us understand that we're individuals. In Eastern thought, the idea is not to focus on the individual self but to realize that each of us is part of a whole, because all beings affect each other and are part of an interdependent web. (One small but profound example: honeybees. They pollinate seventy out of one hundred species of plants that provide people with food. If honeybees were to disappear, so would half the food in our supermarkets.)

So is the ego, or the self, bad? No, not as long as we remember the law of karma: our actions affect others. (You'll learn more about karma in an upcoming chapter.)

pratipaksha bhavana

(prat-i-PAK-sha BAH-va-na)
Replacing negative thoughts
with positive ones.

When disturbed by negative thoughts,
opposite (positive) ones should be thought of.
This is Pratipaksha Bhavana.
—Sutra 2.33, from *The Yoga Sutras of Patanjali*,
translation by Sri Swami Satchidananda

Pratipaksha Bhavana—or the Yoga Thought-Swap Trick, as we called it in yoga teacher training—suffers from a case of mistaken identity: it's often confused with denial. This is understandable, given that Pratipaksha Bhavana encourages us to swap out negative, harmful thoughts for more positive ones. Isn't that some sort of avoidance? Sure, who wouldn't rather be thinking about a beach vacation instead of worrying about losing a job, but is that really helpful?

Yes, because Pratipaksha Bhavana can keep us from falling into a web of obsessive fear that hobbles everything we do. Pratipaksha Bhavana is in alignment with what the Dalai Lama says about worrying: if a problem can be fixed, then there's no need to worry; if a problem can't be fixed, then there's no point to worry. Once you have taken appropriate action to address a situation, tormenting yourself with worst-case-scenario fantasies is painful, useless, and harmful. The English translation of *pratipaksha bhavana* is "moving to the other side of the mansion." (Isn't it lovely to think of your mind as a mansion?) It is a tool that takes you from negative what-if thinking to positive, more creative thinking.

As I write this chapter, I'm sitting in a hospital waiting room as my mother undergoes eye surgery. It's a routine procedure, nothing major, but part of the process was my being assigned as Mom's medical proxy in the event of an emergency. It's unlikely that something will happen, but if it did, I would have to make life-or-death decisions for my mother. It's scary when someone you love is taken down the hall to an operating room, with just a thin paper gown wrapped around them. It's not unusual for both patient and companion to start thinking about those worst-case scenarios, the ones you really don't want to think about.

But after you've done all you can do in a given situation, Pratipaksha Bhavana helps you find balance on your surfboard again with a conscious decision to switch from the negative thoughts that seem to occur automatically to positive thoughts that you can choose to bring to mind and focus on.

As I sit in this hospital waiting room, I remember the first time I used Pratipaksha Bhavana, a long time ago, in another hospital.

"Don't wash off your makeup," Marnie said as I headed for the bathroom.

"Why?" I asked. "It's late, we're going to sleep. Who's going to see me besides you?"

She shifted carefully in her hospital bed, wincing as the big tube leading out of her rib cage moved, but she forced a sly smile. "The doctor who makes the rounds at night is hot and single. His name is Dr. D'Amato; I call him Dr. Tomato. I'm telling you, leave your makeup on."

Marnie and I were having what she billed as a hospital pajama party. She was allowed to have a guest stay overnight in her room while recuperating from massive surgery. The tumor had been removed, along with most of her esophagus. That meant her stomach had to be moved up into her chest, and I felt a little faint when she explained the rest of her rearranged insides. A large tube in her side drained fluid out of her while smaller IVs in her arms put fluid back into her. The only kind of body-invading tube Marnie had any say in was the catheter, and she'd flat-out refused it: "That one's not just painful, it's insulting," she said.

She insisted on using the bathroom as usual, though getting there required a combination of technical skills and choreography. We had to shut off the correct switches on the IV drip machine or it would screech warning beeps. Then we had to disconnect the end of the big tube in her chest from the bag at the side of the bed, get the IV tree, and untangle those tubes.

Then, the hardest part: Marnie's convincing her surgery-riddled body to make a five-step trek across the room. It was so painful for her, even leaning on me the whole way, that once she closed the door I wept for her. I was quick about wiping away my tears before she came out again. She hated to see people cry.

Mascara now smeared, I rolled my eyes at Marnie's hospital matchmaking attempts. "If this hot night doctor is truly worthy, he'll see past my unglamorous face and librarian glasses and fall in love with the real me."

"Of course, absolutely," she said. "Um . . . Maybe just a little tinted lip gloss?"

The hospital had special chairs that folded out into single beds, and I lay on one facing Marnie, watching her breathing. I didn't think she was sleeping; hospitals are terrible places to try to rest. Constant announcements, beeping noises, the night-shift nurses coming in hourly to check her vital signs. Blood pressure, heart rate, IVs, *Anything you need? Okay.* An hour later: blood pressure, heart rate, IVs, refill one bag, empty another, *You doing okay? Good.* Next hour: blood pressure, heart rate . . . An hourly postoperative rosary.

The nurses and hospital noise weren't what kept me awake. They barely registered through the thickness of my increasingly dark thoughts. Technically, Marnie's surgery had been a success, and we should've been able to sigh with relief and scream with joy. But this type of cancer was aggressive and fast moving; it might return. Or it could show up somewhere else. Marnie was now in limbo, a space between possibly going to be okay and possibly not. And "not" meant . . .

Panic's icy grip tightened. *Yoga tools, yoga tools,* I thought, and suddenly I remembered Pratipaksha Bhavana. I shoved the dark thoughts away with better, more hopeful ones. Marnie had a great medical team, and they'd found the tumor and been able to remove it. She had a good shot at recovery. I even managed to smile by recalling her joke about her reorganized insides; she said she'd soon be the girl who would say, "Gee, I'm hungry," and rub her upper chest, where her stomach had been relocated.

"Suz?"

Marnie's voice was the dusky adult voice I knew, but the tone, the plaintiveness of the request, was that of a child reliant on a grown-up for help. "Suz, I'm sorry, I need to go to the bathroom . . ."

She hated asking for help with anything, and now she had to ask for help just to pee. Knowing that pity dug into her worse than the tube sticking out of her rib cage, I teased her: "Again? What, did you sneak a bottle of champagne in your hospital kit or something?" I could tell she didn't notice the tremble in my voice because she was laughing.

The voyage to the bathroom and back was a triumph. As Marnie was easing her wracked body onto the bed, there was a knock at the door. "Dr. D'Amato!" she said, smiling broadly, waggling her eyebrows at me. Before he could begin the vital-signs rosary of blood pressure, heart rate, and all the other checking, she said, "I want you to meet my friend Suzan. Suz, this is Dr. Tomato. Oops, I meant Dr. *D'Amato*, sorry," she said, not sorry at all.

I was about to tell her to skip playing Cupid and let the doctor do what he had to do when that dim gray room became a little brighter with Marnie's exaggerated winks and grin. I'd been wondering how she could possibly think about unimportant things like setting me up with her doctor (who was, as she'd promised, hot) until I remembered Pratipaksha Bhavana. Disturbed by negative thoughts? We were in danger of being ripped apart by all the sharp-clawed possibilities looming in that dark hospital room. But everything that could be done had been, and now, while waiting to see what would be, Marnie just needed a little distraction, switching to fun thoughts that had nothing to do with cancer.

We girl-talked about Dr. Tomato and other silly things for the rest of the night. When the nurses came to do the rosary, Marnie joked with them: "Can I switch to a vodka IV this time, and can you get one for my friend here?" We only stopped laughing to watch the sun as it rose, magical and miraculous, over the river.

Pratipaksha Bhavana had gotten us through a long night of what-ifs. Now we could rest in our focus on the ultimate positive thought: the daily gift of the world being bathed in light.

yoga mind practice:
Pratipaksha Bhavana,
the Yoga Thought-Swap Trick

Franklin D. Roosevelt's saying "The only thing we have to fear is fear itself" was wisdom to be taken as a concrete suggestion. Fear is a smoke alarm: it brings our attention to matters that need to be dealt with, either immediately, as in getting out of the way of physical danger, or in the long term, as with treatment for illness. Fear shows us that there is something that needs our attention.

It's not fear that paralyzes us, but FEAR, or "false evidence appearing real"—the worst-case scenarios we conjure under the guise of preparing ourselves for anything. Instead of helping us take action, though, these FEAR-based thoughts can incapacitate us.

This is where Pratipaksha Bhavana is so useful. It teaches us to use an approach I call Stop and Swap: it stops FEAR-based thoughts and swaps them out for more constructive, positivity-based thinking. The results: We are calmer. We are less stressed and able to make better decisions.

Of course, the hardest time to think of something positive is when you need to the most. That's why it's helpful to learn Pratipaksha Bhavana's Stop and Swap method before you need it, just like learning to use the kitchen fire extinguisher *before* your dinner is flambéing away on the stove. Pratipaksha Bhavana is a fear extinguisher.

There are two ways to have Pratipaksha Bhavana at the ready in case of emergency (which can be any time you're feeling uncomfortable stress).

1. **Visual Meditation**—Do a few rounds of your regular Deergha Swasam yoga breathing practice, then allow your breathing to return to its natural rhythm. Using your creative imagination, expand on the classic guided

meditation instruction to envision your "happy place"—a location where you feel serene. Mine is a peaceful mountaintop, surrounded by fragrant pine trees and flowers, where my husband and I go on our wedding anniversary. Be detailed in your visualization of your comforting place. Bring to mind what you're sitting on, what scents are in the air, what sounds you might hear, whether the temperature is cool or warm. Spend some time there in your mind until you feel calmer. You can also write a description of this place in your Yoga Mind journal to help make it even more vivid.

2. **Mantra Meditation**—After your regular Deergha Swasam practice, give yourself a few minutes to observe your natural breathing rhythm. Then write a Pratipaksha Bhavana list of positive thoughts in your Yoga Mind journal. They can be general statements, such as:

> *I am divinely guided.*
> *I am a divine light.*
> *I breathe in peace and breathe out love.*

Use these, or make up others that suit you.

Know that you have both of these methods available to you whenever disturbing thoughts arise. Again, this is not about ignoring problems; interestingly, the solution you need can present itself during use of Pratipaksha Bhavana, because you're calmer and more receptive to guidance.

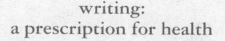

writing:
a prescription for health

Keeping a journal has been shown to reduce stress and improve mental and even physical health. An article published by the University of Rochester says that the simple act of writing down your thoughts can help you manage anxiety and cope with depression by seeing negative thought patterns and prioritizing problems. A study by James Pennebaker, a psychologist and researcher at the University of Texas at Austin, found that patients who did daily writing exercises experienced increases in their immune systems.

A journal like this is a safe space for you to explore your feelings and create positive changes. Don't feel that you have to write in any sort of "formal" way; the pages are for you and don't ever have to be shown to anyone else. Write streams of consciousness, draw, doodle in the margins— pour your true self onto the page! This will be easier after doing a few rounds of three-part breathing. Let your journal be a road map to your soul.

japa

(JAH-pah)
A form of meditation
using repetition of mantra.

When you see people meditating with what looks like a necklace of beads, they're practicing japa: repeating a mantra over and over, either silently or quietly aloud (the Sanskrit word *japa* actually means "muttering"). The beads are used to count repetitions of the mantra. Japa is a way of giving the mind something to focus on during meditation, an anchor for wandering thoughts.

The story told in my yoga teacher training class was that in long-ago times in India, when elephants were ridden or led through markets, their trunks would wander into baskets of fruit, boxes of sweets, wherever something smelled tasty. Clever elephant drivers figured out that if the trunk was occupied, it might not wander so easily. This is why you see elephants in India holding batons in their trunks.

My teachers drew the parallel between the wandering elephants' trunks, always looking for something sweet, and our minds drifting during meditation, always looking for something to think about, and not necessarily something sweet. We can get distracted just as easily by fearful thoughts, the dreaded what-ifs, as we do by pleasant fantasies or memories. Japa keeps the mind focused by giving it a baton in the form of a mantra.

We now know about neuroplasticity, the scientific discovery that the brain is far more able and willing to learn new things, at any age, than we used to believe. One of the keys to learning and cultivating beneficial habits is repetition. New neural pathways—our brain's information highways—are created and strengthened by repeating thoughts and corresponding actions. There is less scientific research on the effects of repeated thoughts on our emotions, though you can do your own study by reaching into your own personal experiences.

When I wanted to learn how to draw again, I took lessons from Sketchbook Skool, an online art school made up of teachers and students from all over the world. Many of the students and even faculty members say that as children, they were uninhibited, happy artists—until a teacher or parent criticized their work. In many cases, this stopped them from drawing entirely. It took years, even decades, for them to draw again.

The mind and body are hardwired to avoid pain, even when it's emotional rather than physical. You hear criticism, your emotions register pain, and it may even manifest as physical pain, such as the nauseated feeling some people experience during arguments. One of my teachers at Integral Yoga, Kali Morse, always refers to "the mind-body," because you cannot affect one without affecting the other. At the start of her class, she'll ask the students, "How are the mind-bodies today?" The body and mind are inextricably linked.

The mind-body feels this pain and will go out of its way to avoid experiencing it again. That neural pathway is strengthened every time you think about it. The result? The people who wanted to draw avoided making art for years. If somehow they'd found a way to push through and draw, they still had lingering doubts about their talents and abilities.

The doubts lasted until, that is, they began listening to different messages and repeating them back to themselves. The teachers and student community told them that they could draw, so they tried it, and their efforts were met with positive reinforcement. They repeated the new behavior and received more encouragement. They began to think believable things: *I can get good at this.* Or simply, *I can.* The more they told themselves the positive messages, the more they believed them, and the stronger the new neural pathways became.

I was one of these students. I was apparently talented enough to get into a school for artists, where the teachers tried to prepare us for careers in creative fields. This usually took the form of pointing out our mistakes and failures without the balance of encouraging our attempts and successes. Thin-skinned, I withered with every critique. I barely graduated, and I did not draw again until a few years ago. Whenever I hear someone explain why they stopped doing something they once enjoyed with, "Well, my teacher told me I had no talent . . . ," or "I can't dance—my husband once said I'm a klutz . . . ," I marvel with dismay at the profound effect of negative messages—usually just opinions—that we mistake for facts.

Yet that effect is encouraging, because it means the opposite must also be true. The more we tell ourselves something positive, the stronger and more ingrained that thought becomes. Eventually, we can manifest it as truth.

Japa was designed to give meditators a point of focus to keep their minds from wandering. My interpretation of japa is that it is an excellent tool for paving over old, usually untrue stories and current fears with positive messages that, with repetition, solidify into beliefs. Then we can act on those beliefs, and our actions turn beliefs into facts.

I've told you about Francesco's mantra, *When I get better.* He didn't specifically say he was going to form a mantra, but he said *When I get better* so many times, he came to believe he would get better—and he did. His perspective shifted from fear-based depression to open-minded optimism. That optimism can then become reality.

This has also been my experience with an affirmation-style japa practice. A few years ago, I found myself going through a period of depression. This happens to me and, I imagine, a lot of people from time to time; there was no external trigger, nothing that would explain it, and that made it even scarier. I found darkness expanding within me, inhibiting first my ability to work, then my ability to enjoy things that typically made me very happy. I stopped drawing, then writing. Over time I stopped wanting even to leave the house to go for a walk. The process was slow and subtle, and, although in my case not acute enough to be dangerous, certainly no way to lose precious days.

At that time I came across a book called *May Cause Miracles* by Gabrielle Bernstein. She was very big on affirmations and encouraged repeating them at certain points during the day. I took this suggestion a step further and turned the affirmations into japa meditations, repeating them over and over. I did this the first thing in the morning, and what a great way to start the day; not only did this practice give my mind a point of focus for meditation, it strengthened the messages until they became strong and solid beliefs.

Sanskrit mantras are said to have sound vibrations that affect you even when repeated silently, even if you don't know what you're saying. Whether you repeat phrases in an ancient language or in modern English, affirmations as japa meditation are an unbeatable tool for casting aside what is old, likely untrue, and definitely no longer useful, and finding the radiant light of truth within you.

yoga mind practice:
Affirmations as Japa Meditation

Japa meditation is a wonderful answer to those who say they don't know how to meditate because they can't clear their minds. With japa, you don't have to; the goal of your meditation is to give your mind something to do—in this case, repeating a mantra.

172 ❋ Suzan Colón

Back on day four, you chose a personal mantra. For your practice that begins today and continues through the rest of this program, and, I hope, beyond, you can use that mantra or choose a new one.

As with Francesco's personal message about getting better, a mantra can be most effective when positively framed and spacious enough for possibilities we can't imagine. For example, instead of saying *I will lose twenty pounds*, your mantra could be *This body is a divine temple.* This message would trigger the feeling that you are honoring your body right now, not in an imagined future. (Your body truly is miraculous, no matter how you might want it to be different than it is now.) Honoring yourself feels good. This feeling of self-respect and reverence could lead you to find an asana practice you like doing and to eat healthy food, which you can think of as offerings to the temple your soul resides in. A mantra with a spacious message of positivity and love can manifest in a variety of ways.

If your work with the yoga tools has revealed some obstacles on your path, you can direct your mantra toward that. If you're going through a difficult time and find yourself in fear, choose a mantra that will bring you into a calmer place while acknowledging what you are going through. Or maybe all is well and you could just use an upbeat thought to start your day off joyously. Whichever category you're in, you can write your own mantra, or choose from this list:

I am a divine light.

I am divinely guided.

I breathe in love; I breathe out compassion.

There is a river of peace within me.

Om shanti, shanti, shanti [Om peace, peace, peace].

This body is a divine temple.

I am aligned with Spirit mind.

I release what no longer serves me and invite what helps me serve.

I am serenity.

I am a channel of Spirit's love.

Once you've chosen a mantra or have formed one of your own, sit for your daily Deergha Swasam practice. When, after a moment or two of conscious three-part breathing, you have returned to normal breathing, begin repeating your mantra to yourself, either silently or quietly aloud. Don't worry about syncing your mantra to your breath, unless that works without altering your natural, comfortable breathing pattern.

Some parts of your mind may want to argue with the mantra; just gently return to the mantra. This isn't a debate or a discussion. It's a meditation.

Write your mantra in your Yoga Mind journal, as well as the feelings you experienced during the meditation. If you're partial to writing, you can also try an interesting variation I learned while on retreat at Integral Yoga's ashram in Virginia: written japa meditation, where you write your mantra over and over. It's a very interesting experience, and you're then receiving the message through thought and in writing.

Do your japa practice for three to five minutes this morning, longer if you want, and continue it every day for the duration of your Yoga Mind practice—and beyond, if it works for you. You can also repeat it at midday for a few minutes, at night before you go to sleep, and of course, whenever you feel stress.

day 19

samskaras

(sahm-SKAR-as)
Repeating cycles of behaviors.

*If you do not pour water on your plant, what will happen? It will
slowly wither and die. Our habits will also slowly wither and die
away if we do not give them an opportunity to manifest. You need not
fight to stop a habit. Just don't give it an opportunity to repeat itself.*
—Swami Satchidananda

For a long time during my study of yoga, I thought samskaras were like the movie *Groundhog Day*, starring negative behavior. At the yoga studio, some of the students would
talk about how they kept doing things they didn't want to do,
like eating things they'd sworn off of or smoking. The teacher
listening would nod and say, "Samskaras. You're in a cycle."

According to yogic philosophy, samskaras, or cycles of behavior, come with us from past lives. (I personally have never had a

sense of a past life. The current one is more than enough for me to handle.) We keep repeating these patterns over and over until we learn from them, and then—at last!—we achieve moksha, or liberation from the cycle. The idea of repeating behaviors again and again, over lifetimes, made me regard samskaras with fear. As I learned more about them, though, I came to view them with respect, and even gratitude.

My own version of a samskara was the on-again, off-again relationship I was in at the time I was in teacher training. I didn't see it as an unhealthy pattern. I thought if we (meaning *he*) could just make some changes, we (meaning *I*) would be fine. My list was long. "If he could just open his mind to commitment, if he could only be more ambitious, if he'd only be more sociable," I pined yet again to a friend.

"So basically," she said, "if he could just become a completely different person." That's about what I was asking of him.

He and I discussed our sticking points endlessly. We compromised, we gave in, we got angry, we fought, we broke up, we missed each other and the good parts of the relationship, we got back together, and we would go through a briefly happy period before something would come up and set us off. Then the cycle would start all over again.

When we're in a samskara, it's hard to see it. As my friend Alice puts it, "You can't see the picture if you're in the frame." We tell ourselves that something about this time is different. We *really* mean it now, or we believe that the other person does. Or we swear that *this is it*. Or this time we blame it on someone or something else. Then the snake eats its tail again and, like Bill Murray's character in *Groundhog Day*, we realize that nothing around us has changed. That's because we are the ones who need to change.

The first new thing I learned about samskaras is that they're not scary purgatories of punishment for "bad" behavior. They're teachers. Like fear, samskaras are smoke alarms, drawing our attention to habits and reactions that need to evolve. Samskaras occur with the goal of prompting svadhyaya, self-study, provoking questions: *Do you see the result of this action? How do you feel? Not too good? Are you ready to make a change?*

That different way of thinking about samskaras, as teachers, led to my second realization: they're not all negative. Samskaras are defined as repeated behaviors, not exclusively harmful ones. It's just that we don't talk about our good habits as much as our bad ones. In fact, the only time we really talk about habits and behaviors is around December and January, the time we're conditioned to make New Year's resolutions. Then the focus is all on the bad behavior we'll swear off of and the saintly, perfect behavior we promise we'll take up.

The lessons samskaras had for me got lost in fits of self-condemnation and oaths that I would achieve perfection in an imagined future. My focus was on beating myself up for being late to work again, cheating on diets, drowning my sorrows too much, not meditating enough. This only fed the cycle, and I'd boomerang back with higher expectations and harder falls. Samskaras asked me to take a less ego-centered view: *I* was not damaged or weak, but the behavior, and the repetition, meant there was an issue I needed to address appropriately. Viewing the samskaras as teachers helped me see the lessons and make healthy changes. *See this cycle. This became a habit over time. Don't get sidetracked by shame; become open to change.*

Next, I focused on positive samskaras. Meeting with Francesco had become a regular habit interrupted only by his journeys to participate in studies and treatment around the country and the globe, but visiting him regularly was a cycle that benefited us both. Other good habits: I routinely met my work deadlines, and flossing every night had to count for something. Those repeating behaviors helped me view myself with more of a sense of balance.

Some lessons were learned more quickly than others. I did return to my samskara relationship again, but this time I understood it as a cycle trying to show me something. What I found was fear. Francesco's accident and Marnie's diagnosis of a potentially terminal illness had removed the ground from under my feet. Their treatment, ongoing over months, meant there was no immediate resolution. I lived in a constant state of hope and desperation. And so I looked for something solid and familiar, even when the familiar could no longer be confused for comfortable. Although I wasn't ready to release this particular cycle just yet, becoming aware of the samskara, and my willingness to see its lesson for me, helped make me receptive to change.

yoga mind practice:
The Three Steps of Samskaras

The sign of being caught in a negative samskara is a heavy sigh, followed by "Here I am again." If you find yourself engaging in behaviors you previously swore you wouldn't repeat, you're in a cycle that will likely play out again until you see the lesson the samskara is trying to show you.

The lesson is not some form of punishment by pain; pain is the result of the actions, not an instructive lesson in itself. Nor is the lesson that you are some sort of bad or damaged person, which is simply untrue. You are human. Human beings make mistakes. One of the keys to lasting happiness is learning from our mistakes so we can grow and become better versions of ourselves. We become happier, and we also become more useful; our example is instructive to those around us.

The lesson your samskara is trying to show you is that something is behind the repeated behavior, and that trigger can be addressed. As I mentioned before, I was repeatedly late for work, yet always on time for pleasurable things such as dates with friends. My lateness wasn't due to external issues like my alarm clock, or the bus or train or weather or wardrobe malfunctions. Those might have been the issue once or twice, but more than that meant I had to take ownership. (That alone was empowering; it dismantled the idea that I was the helpless victim of some kind of bad karma.)

Looking without judgment, I saw that I was the cause of my lateness, and I became willing to see the truth behind the behavior: I had anxiety about my performance at work. Once I addressed that with meditation and pranayama, the lateness issue went away. I was on time, and I was less anxious and did better work.

Sometimes the trigger is not so easily identified, and it may never become clear. In that case, you use the manifestation of the cycle to find a solution. A colleague of mine was a heavy smoker, especially when he became stressed out. He joined a group of people working toward cessation of reliance on cigarettes. This community understood him and his habit. He met with them weekly and, when stressed, began calling them instead of reaching for cigarettes, and over time, he was able to quit smoking. He never really found out the reason for his smoking, but he and his new friends formed a sangha and worked on a solution together. He has been smoke-free for over ten years.

Turn your negative cycles into beneficial teachers with the Three Steps of Samskaras. Begin with your regular three-part yoga breathing practice. Allow your breathing to become normal. Let yourself relax into the rhythm of your breath for a moment or two, easing into the willingness to ask yourself if there are any repeating patterns in your life that are causing you harm.

If you find something, follow these three steps within your meditation:

1. **Look at it.** Don't get caught up in the outward manifestation of your repeated cycles of behavior, or in feelings of guilt or shame. That's not what samskaras are about. Explore underneath the behavior and find what is motivating it. It may or may not become clear, but usually it involves fear, stress, or something unresolved.

2. **Learn from it.** See what the samskara is trying to teach you. A student of mine was a consistent yes-man at work, until a new boss challenged him to give his honest opinions about company initiatives. He was

reluctant, to the point that he was losing his standing in the company, not to mention his self-respect. By looking for the satya, the truth, of his tendency to agree, he saw a childhood full of submissive behavior carved by domineering parents and school bullies. By observing this without judgment, this student saw how his behavior came about and that now, as an adult, it no longer applied to his current life.

3. **Let go.** Make peace with the samskara. Understand that in some way, at some time, the behavior may have served you. This is another way to keep from being distracted by judgment and unnecessary shame. Thank the samskara for the lessons it has taught you, and let it know you are prepared to release it. This process may take time, but once you have learned the lesson, you can't un-know it. You will see that it no longer serves you. Gradually, you will release your grip on it. As a mudra, or symbolic gesture, open your hands to release the samskara and receive the new gift: moksha, or freedom.

addictions and yoga

If the samskara you've discovered is an addiction, and the cycles of behavior are bringing about harmful, even life-threatening results, you will be taking the bravest and most spiritually correct action by seeking help. Remember, you don't have to be a patient at your local hospital to ask for assistance in finding appropriate programs, such as Alcoholics Anonymous or other twelve-step groups that address your specific needs. Know that there is help waiting for you, and kind, compassionate people ready to guide you to and through these programs. Twelve-step groups cost nothing, but they can give people their lives back.

Throughout my time as a yoga teacher, I've met more than a few people who say they believe yoga will "fix" their addiction problem. I've also met people who stop taking their antidepressants or other prescribed medication because they think they don't need it anymore now that they're doing yoga. I have seen the miracles that yoga can bring about for people—*in conjunction* with treatment that directly addresses issues that could seriously compromise their health. Yoga is an excellent support system for Western medicine, recovery from addiction and alcoholism, physical therapy, depression, and more. It works best *with*, not instead of, appropriate treatment.

Due to a reclassification of opiate-based painkillers—which have the same basic ingredients as heroin—drug addiction has spread across this country in previously unseen numbers. People who have no prior history of addiction find themselves in the shocking circumstances of hard-core addicts, and many are dying. The statistics for addiction are particularly high for women over forty. Again, if you suspect that you or someone you care about is suffering from addiction or alcoholism, the best action you can take is seeking help. Then you can add yoga to your recovery program for extra well-being. See the appendix at the back of this book for resources.

day 20

dhayana

(DYE-ana)

A steady flow of attention toward an object,
such as your breathing,
your mantra, or a sacred image.

I don't think I can meditate," Francesco said.

Fresh snow was falling amid the branches of the trees out-side his window. Francesco had returned from the stem cell surgery in China, and as soon as he was able, we resumed his breathing practices. We'd started out with three minutes and were now work-ing up to ten, with pauses for silence. If he was feeling depressed or tense, he would imagine inhaling love and exhaling fear. Francesco's ability to concentrate was admirable, and I suggested we try a little longer, with more silence, to turn his pranayama practice into a meditation. But he wasn't sure. "I can't meditate," he insisted. "I can't make my mind blank. I think too much."

This is the response I've always heard to the suggestion of meditation. People may not even know what meditation is, but they're certain they won't be able to do it. "I can't clear my mind" is the primary perceived obstacle for would-be meditators, even more than not having the time to meditate.

But meditation isn't about turning your mind into a blank slate. I learned what it really is from a genuine swami. As Francesco listened, I told him about a pivotal day in my yoga training where I experienced a revelation that changed my relationship to meditation forever.

The swami sat wrapped in orange robes, his legs crossed in half-lotus position. His face radiated the kind of serene joy and inner peace that makes people want to meditate in the first place. Swami Ramananda was speaking to my yoga teacher training group about meditation. We were all paying particularly close attention because he had once been like us—a regular American from a typical family. He hadn't been raised on an ashram in India, though he did now live and work at Integral Yoga's ashram in San Francisco, where he served as president. Apparently, learning how to meditate was part of what gave Ramananda that inner glow that translated to such outer kindness. The students couldn't help but want to scoot a tad closer to him on their floor cushions to bask in a little of that sunshine.

"Any questions about meditation?" he asked after his lecture.

There was a pause before a hesitant hand went up. "I can't meditate," the teacher trainee admitted. "I have too many thoughts zooming around in my head." We all nodded, feeling relieved that we weren't the only ones with this problem. "No matter how hard I try," the student said, "I just can't seem to clear my mind."

"Yes," Ramananda said, nodding. "Neither can I."

We collectively jaw-dropped while he continued. "When I sit down to meditate, I have all these thoughts about my to-do list, people I have to call back and email, meetings, things that need to be done around the ashram . . ." The swami shrugged. "It just never seems to end, does it?"

Some of us gave a little head-shake of disbelief, both about a swami having a to-do list (who knew?) and the other, more important part. "Wait," another student said. "You're a swami— a monk who renounced all worldly possessions so you could dedicate yourself to yoga. You live in an ashram and meditate for long periods of time, a couple of times a day." Ramananda nodded. "But you just said you can't clear your mind," the student went on. "Then . . . how do you meditate?"

Ramananda's laugh was one of gentle agreement. "Meditation isn't about clearing your mind," he said. He went on to explain that this isn't even possible. Our minds were designed to gather information and calculate and solve problems. That was a matter of life and death in the days when we had to gather food and could be charged by an animal, and even today, it's still important. But there's a difference between getting caught up in thoughts, and just having a thought and then going back to observing your breath, if you're doing a breathing meditation, or repeating your mantra, if you're doing Japa meditation.

"Think of it this way," he said, seeing our confused but eager expressions. "You're sitting on a rock in the middle of a beautiful, still lake, and occasionally, you slide off the rock and into the water. Meditation," he said, "is getting back up on that warm, sunny rock."

I think all of our minds did actually go blank in that instant of learning what seemed like the secret of the universe: meditation is not about clearing the mind, but about returning, time after nonjudgmental time, to gently concentrating on an object. There is a word for this focused flow of attention: dhayana.

A stream may course over stones and around twists and bends, but that doesn't interrupt its flow. Thoughts are like the stones and twists; the stream of concentration is dhayana. It may be interrupted, but like that stream, it returns to its course. The only time it can be stopped is if it gets dammed up, like when we get caught up in thoughts that distract us from what we were focusing on.

Just this knowledge alone can keep that from happening. We don't have to be distracted by layers of thinking—having a thought, then berating ourselves for having the thought and "not being able to meditate," then having other thoughts on top of that. Meditation, as Swami Ramananda said, is simply observing that you're having a thought and returning to your point of focus, whether it's your gentle inhalation and exhalation in breathing meditation, each step of a walking meditation, or a visualization of climbing back up on that warm, sunny rock.

This liberating perspective of what meditation can be trains us to be present in each moment. After Francesco's surgery, the rigorous stay in a different country, and the long journey home, he was now in a stressful waiting game, wondering what effect the treatment might have on him, if any. The question weighed heavily on his mind, and it was worthy of its weight. Likewise, Marnie and everyone who loved her were holding a collective breath while waiting for the next check-in with her oncology team. We each have our weight to carry—worry about someone or a situation, waiting for news, something we can't fix or hurry along.

Through focus, and the single, simple goal of returning to the object of focus, dhayana teaches us to stay present, moment to moment, both within meditation and outside of meditation, in daily life. Dhayana trains you to focus on your cup of tea, your child's smile, your dog's wagging tail. It can't take away whatever weighs on you, but being in the moments that bring the opportunity for a deep breath, maybe even a smile, helps us to bear that weight.

yoga mind practice:
Flowing Focus

Today's practice is dhayana, the steady flow of meditative attention. First, choose an object to focus on during meditation: your breathing; japa, repetition of your mantra; or the visual meditation from your Pratipaksha Bhavana practice.

Next, find a comfortable seat. Sitting on a chair is absolutely fine if that is what your body prefers.

Begin your Deergha Swasam practice and continue breathing in three parts for a few rounds. Then allow your breathing to find its own natural, comfortable pattern, without doing anything to alter it. Focus on your breathing, repetition of a mantra, or visualization. Remember, your mind *will* wander; that's not a failure or lack of skill, just the nature of the mind. When thoughts come up, notice that you're thinking and gently return to your meditation focus. This is kind of like watching traffic from the street corner; just as there's no need to walk into the traffic, there's no need to get involved in the thoughts. Or, if you like knitting, think of it this way: A thought is like a ball of yarn. Getting caught up in thoughts is knitting, actively working the thoughts. Just let the ball of yarn sit there and return to your focus.

Meditate for anywhere from five to ten minutes, or more, if you're comfortable.

tiliksha

(tih-TEEK-shah)
The capacity for enduring difficulties,
and the strength that comes from
knowing you can endure.

Long ago, the Buddha was speaking in a small town, sharing what he'd learned about freedom from suffering, when a woman suddenly rushed up to him holding the body of her child. Through wrenching sobs, the woman, Kisa Gotami, begged the Buddha to bring her child back to life. This was at a time when people were unsure of whether the Buddha, because he had become enlightened, was a man or a god.

The Buddha spoke gently with Kisa. He told her that her child could come back to life if she found a mustard seed from a home that had known no pain of loss from death. Kisa ran from house to house, and she heard story after story of loss—of parents and elder relatives, children, friends, teachers, and others. The people wept over these losses, but they also smiled when telling Kisa stories about the people they'd loved.

As the day ended, the sun setting over the village, Kisa returned to the Buddha with an understanding that everyone is touched by loss. With the help of the villagers, Kisa laid her child to rest. She was in deep pain, but her suffering in grief's isolation was over.

The story is meant to convey the truth that death is part of the fabric of life, and each of us will experience loss. What I also found in the story is titiksha, the strength within us that helps us endure the darkest sorrows.

There is the road to loss, and the road after. Sometimes loss comes quickly. Other times, loss drags its feet in a reluctant march forward. Anyone who has helped someone they love through an ongoing illness knows each long and heavy step of that march.

During Marnie's illness, the days went from hopeful to hollow to unbearable. All of us around her kept going, showing up at the hospital with food, with a good story, with tear-soggy tissues hidden in our sleeves, with big smiles or more honest faces, with work from the office, with overnight kits and pajamas. And with titiksha, our capacity to endure our fears and be strong for our friend, daughter, wife.

There were many times I didn't think I could keep being strong for Marnie. One afternoon I thought I'd fall apart if I went to the hospital, and I wondered whether it would be better for her if I stayed home. Something in me kept my feet moving forward in that heavy march, though. By the time I got to the hospital, where Marnie lay looking like a skeleton, I'd pulled myself together and breezed in, telling her she wouldn't believe what some celebrity had gone and done now.

When put to the test, we endure. Even when we're sure we can't, we do. We may think we have no choice, that we have to endure the chemo or the fear for the person we love who's receiving it, but we do have a choice: We could run. Not show up. Break down and hide.

But showing up when you're at your breaking point, and before and after, is titiksha. When you think you're at your weakest, you'll find out you're stronger than you've ever been. The inner strength that allows you to bear the weight you're carrying, even and especially when you think you can't, is titiksha.

The Bhagavad Gita, one of the most important spiritual texts ever written, tells the story of a warrior named Arjuna who, through a long and complicated series of events worthy of a TV drama, has to battle people who were once his friends, his mentors, even his relatives. This celebrated warrior's response to the challenge: a total breakdown, right there on the battlefield. He goes to his chariot and falls apart, unable to face the duty that will liberate his homeland from rule by oppressive despots.

But Arjuna prays and receives guidance from his higher power, Krishna, and he carries out his work. He's in anguish, he doesn't want to fight this battle—but he transcends his personal feelings. "Arjuna endures his own pain and fear for the greater good," Swami Asokananda told the assembled group of teacher trainees during a Bhagavad Gita study course.

"But he *has* to endure," a student said. "He has no choice."

The swami shook his head. "He was ready to give up. He could've walked away. But he found titiksha, the capacity to bear great pain and suffering that is within each of us."

Until that point I'd thought endurance was its own kind of suffering. Yet in yoga philosophy, endurance is a form of strength. Titiksha says that we each have within us not only the capacity to endure but the *strength* to endure.

This is incredibly empowering. Titiksha means it's no accident that we can find reserves within ourselves to keep going during challenges that we might have sworn we couldn't handle before actually being put to the test. This is spiritual design. We feel pain, and we feel it may break us—and it might.

Marnie was surrounded by her family and closest friends the night she died. We stood around her bed and held her hands so she was not alone as she made her passage. Marnie had been in great pain and fear for most of her illness, and her suffering was coming to an end. All that was left was her physical presence going through the motions of breathing, with longer pauses in between each breath.

Her eyes stayed open, refusing to close or look away. That was Marnie.

After she left the body (the yoga term for a person passing from the physical realm to another; yogis don't believe the spirit can die), I fell apart. I made it through the memorial service with some measure of dignity, and then I went home and dismantled my life with the precise skill of a wrecking ball. I overslept, overindulged, and spent an inordinate amount of time in pajamas.

Then I came to. I realized that I was doing a tremendous disservice to my friend by wasting precious time this way. I got dressed. I cleaned up. I went back to work and to my yoga mat. I was a mess, but gradually, painfully, I pulled myself back together. Things that are broken can be repaired.

When I learned about titiksha, I saw how something within, some inner strength, had kept me together during the crucial time Marnie needed help, and that this inner strength also put me back together afterward, piece by piece. Something within Francesco made him shine that huge smile at people at a time when he was still in shock from what had happened to him.

Yes, there are things in life we must endure. As Kisa Gotami learned, loss will touch each of us. But it's titiksha, the strength within each of us, that gives us the ability to endure it.

yoga mind practice:
Find Your Inner Strength with Titiksha

Your exercise today is to look at your own strength, which you find by recalling your weakest moments.

Don't be afraid to do this. You're focusing on strength, and the exercise will be uplifting.

Begin with your yoga breathing practice. After a few rounds of three-part breath, allow your breathing to find its own natural rhythm. Rest your awareness on each inhalation and exhalation for a few moments.

Gradually bring to mind a difficult time in your life. At some point, maybe more than once, you've been, as a friend calls it, "broken down to the ground." You may have lost someone or something very important to you. You, or someone you love, may have become ill, or experienced some other kind of challenge.

Don't dwell on the event. By this point your practice with yoga tools has taught you how to view the past as an observer. The goal in this practice is not to relive painful memories but to discover a vital part of that time you may have missed: titiksha, your inner strength.

If you're reading this, you made it through that difficult time. Or, if your challenge is occurring now, you're showing up. You're here. How did you get here? Titiksha. You may be aware of your own strength and celebrate it, or you may not even have noticed that you were being strong, even when you felt most afraid.

You have endured. You are enduring.

That is the focus of the titiksha practice—notice your capacity for endurance, and see it for what it really is: strength.

Write about your titiksha in your Yoga Mind journal. Look in wonder at your own titiksha, your own strong capacity for endurance, because knowing you have this innate strength will serve you well the next time you experience loss or someone close to you is suffering. Titiksha empowers you at a time when you need it most.

day 22

tapas

(TAHP-ahs)
Viewing painful experiences
as opportunities to
learn and grow.

That which does not kill us makes us stronger.
—Friedrich Nietzsche

Turn all mishaps into the path.
—Buddhist teaching

When Francesco was still in the hospital, he was visited by a small group of people who had come to tell him he would have a life beyond his accident. He might not be able to see that now, they said, but over time his outlook would improve, and possibilities that were hidden behind the fact of the wheelchair would become more apparent. Francesco couldn't quite see it at the time, but he listened to these people because they were in his position, literally: each had a spinal cord injury, and each spoke to him from a wheelchair. They could tell him how things would be because they'd traveled that road themselves.

What was more, they said, after their accidents, they'd learned things about themselves that they'd never known before: how strong and resilient they could be, that their relationships could be deeper and more meaningful. This way of looking at what had happened to them is tapas, learning and growing from painful experiences.

One of the main reasons support groups are so helpful is identification, where one person relates to someone else in the same circumstances. Francesco could hardly take the word of doctors who told him to "move on" when they were in the comfortable position of standing in front of him on their own working legs and able to move as they wished. But he could listen to the people who came to visit him because they'd been where he was. They'd been through the pain and the massive readjustment to a new way of life. They understood exactly how he felt because they'd had the same experiences.

These people, and others who share their experiences in support groups of all kinds, understand tapas. The Sanskrit root of the word, *tap*, means "to burn"; the meaning of tapas is a dedication to growing from painful experiences. In other words, we learn from the burn.

The people who came to talk to Francesco had, at some point in their recovery process, remembered how terrified they'd been when first waking up in the hospital and finding they could no longer feel their legs, or most of their bodies. They remembered the frustration of physical therapy, the nightmares they had after their accidents, the anger—why had this happened to them? Remembering how they'd felt, they sought to bring some measure of comfort to others waking up to new, dramatically altered lives, as they had. They went into the spinal cord injury wings of the hospitals and shared their experiences with the new patients. Sometimes the newly injured people didn't want to hear anything about life in a wheelchair. The visitors understood that, too.

The people who came to visit Francesco and others in the spinal cord injury wing of the hospital, and people in cancer support groups, twelve-step recovery groups, and other sanghas based on the sharing of personal experience, know the gift of tapas. They learned valuable things about themselves from their experiences. They likely felt with raw openness every bit of the pain of what they'd been through, physically, emotionally, mentally, spiritually. They could have stayed with the pain and allowed it to stop them, to stunt and poison them, and perhaps for a while they did.

Yet at some point they made a decision to use the experience as a catalyst for transformation. Lessons were seen and embraced, then shared with others so that they might have some comfort, eventually some healing. In helping others, they were helped, too. This is tapas in action. Pain by itself is just pain. The lessons that can be learned from pain, and shared to help alleviate the suffering of others, are the gold found after the dross is burned away.

A few years after Marnie became ill, I was given an assignment to write about how important it is for caregivers to take care of themselves, too. Each of the experts I interviewed repeated the same advice: finding a support group of people who were going through similar experiences was key to bearing up during life challenges—not only for the people going through the illness or life-altering events, but for the people around them, especially those in caregiving positions. Previously I'd thought that support groups were only for people undergoing treatment for cancer, or who'd had a catastrophic accident or finally hit bottom on alcohol or drugs. I hadn't realized there were also support groups for their families and friends.

Tapas gives pain a purpose. We can become lost in the pain, or we can learn who we truly are in going through it, as metallurgists find gold through the process of burning. After a trial by fire, tapas helps you find the gold within you.

yoga mind practice:
Learn from the Burn of Tapas

This exercise may be somewhat uncomfortable at first, but by the end of the practice, those feelings will be transformed into empowering strength.

Yesterday, you wrote in your Yoga Mind journal about a time or event when your strength, and maybe even your faith, was tested, and you found your titiksha, the inner strength that helped you to endure. Today's exercise is similar. Again, it's not about reliving painful memories, but about finding hidden gold within you.

Do your regular Deergha Swasam practice, releasing into normal breathing after a few rounds. Ease into pranayama meditation, focusing on your inhalations and exhalations for a few minutes. Release the meditation and, in your Yoga Mind journal, write down what you learned from the event you recalled yesterday. These can be things you discovered about yourself that you never knew before, like how strong you can be. They can be things you learned about others, such as how thoughtful people are in times of difficulty. They can be things you would do differently—how you would manage stress, modes of self-care you would implement. Write what you would share if you had a friend going through a similar event.

If you like, share your tapas lessons in the Spiritual Surfer Sangha on Facebook and email them to me to share on my blog at info@suzancolon.net. In sharing our stories and our strength with others, we help one another to be strong.

svadhyaya

(svad-HYA-ya)
Learning about yourself
through introspective study.

You may have discovered something recently: you're not the person you thought you were.

For the past few weeks, you've been using a new set of tools that have helped you learn things about yourself. Satya has helped you see truth. You now know how to look at your samskaras, your repeating cycles of behavior. You were able to do that because of maitri, kindness. Did you know you could be kind to yourself before this, even while doing challenging self-examination? That may be new.

There are many goals to walking a spiritual path, among them discovering who we really are and becoming who we want to be. We do this through the process of svadhyaya, learning about ourselves through introspective study.

Svadhyaya is consciously looking at who you are—your true identity—and recognizing that your identity is not based on labels that come with circumstances. After *Mademoiselle* magazine, where I met Francesco, folded, I thought, *I am unemployed.* "I am" is a very powerful phrase; it speaks to the core, whether we want it to or not. After a while I felt as if the more I said, "I am unemployed," the longer I'd stay that way.

Through svadhyaya, I saw that I was the same person I'd been before the job. I'd learned things and experienced the enhancement of meeting and working with wonderful people, but it wasn't as though I hadn't existed before the job. So instead, I began saying, "I'm looking for work," or "I'm self-employed." That was the truth, and it left a lot of room for possibilities.

I felt more optimistic and ran with it. I began thinking of myself as being in a new business: me. Until I found steady employment, I was the CEO of Me LLC. Even after I found a job, I thought of it as working *with* a company, not *for* them. That way, if something changed, I wouldn't feel as though I'd lost part of my identity.

The change from recognizing that I was not my job or my circumstances helped me conjure the moxie to seek out work. As anyone who has had to look for a job knows, it takes a lot of energy and persistence to keep going. Thinking of myself in this way, as a whole person regardless of what job I had, was empowering. Svadhyaya had revealed my completeness, resilience, open-mindedness, and willingness to keep going despite fear.

It took a while, but I found another job. Years later, when the recession of 2008 came and I was laid off again, I remembered what svadhyaya had shown me. I was able to find regular freelance work, and over time I decided to run my own business (*At least that way*, I thought, *I can't get laid off!*). By using the tool of svadhyaya to learn more about myself, I was able to feel good about myself.

As you peel temporary circumstances and false ideas apart from truth, you begin to see a much more authentic and honest version of you than before. The paradox with svadhyaya is that the new self you discover may be the person you have always been at heart.

I saw this in Francesco's journey through his injury. When I first met him, he had a worldliness about him from traveling and experiencing many different cultures, but he also had an optimism generally associated with youth and innocence. Like many people fresh out of college, he wasn't exactly sure what he wanted to do with his life, and that was fine with him. All he saw ahead were opportunities. When we met at *Mademoiselle*, Fran and I both thought of work as what you did at an office from nine to five. I'm not sure either of us knew that *work* could mean "one's purpose in the world."

When our jobs at *Mademoiselle* ended, Fran was headed toward a career in public relations, a fine and fun path for a twenty-three-year-old. He figured he'd see what happened from there.

After the accident, his view of what his life might look like changed drastically, with a suddenness that turned a vast sky of opportunities into a brick wall. His lack of mobility meant a traditional job in an office was out of the question. His need for care required staying close to home. His options went from limitless to severely limited.

At times he wasn't sure how he would carry on, or even what *not* carrying on would look like. And although situations and circumstances don't define us, they do give us opportunities to find out what we're made of.

Francesco found his titiksha, his ability to endure. He would look at his family and set a sankalpa to keep going, driven by love for them. And through this process of svadhyaya, he found his old optimism.

In quiet moments, even while despairing, deep down he found his natural hopefulness. Now it was different—changed by tapas, what he'd learned from experiences, his positive, open-minded nature had matured and become stronger. Fran was realistic; he wasn't going to say he could do *anything* he wanted, but he couldn't take to heart the idea that there was *nothing* he could do. That wouldn't help, and it wasn't what his true self believed. He wasn't sure what his future was going to look like now, but he was willing to become open-minded about it. "I don't know" went from being a scary thought to an empowering idea.

Svadhyaya, the gathering of knowledge through introspection, helps us find our true selves. It can show an old aspect of ourselves in a new light, how we are transformed by a situation, or how we can transform a situation—even when we are seemingly at our most powerless.

Chris Rosati was a thirty-nine-year-old husband and father when he was diagnosed with Lou Gehrig's disease, or ALS. The disease is incurable and terminal, and as it progresses it robs people of their mobility, their capacity to speak, and eventually their ability to breathe on their own.

Yet Chris came to think of himself as the luckiest man alive. His situation gave him an immeasurable appreciation for his family and his life. Given three years to live, and eventually confined to a wheelchair, Chris decided he wanted to spend his remaining time finding a way to make people smile. His big idea: steal a truck full of Krispy Kreme donuts and give them away.

Clearly, there were a few issues with this plan, but Chris decided to put it out there anyway. The universe answered. He was soon aided and abetted in his caper by Krispy Kreme, which gave him a bus packed with donuts to give out at Chris's old high school. His joy was even greater than the kids' collective sugar high. Over time, and after a few more busloads of donuts, Chris launched Inspire MEdia, a foundation dedicated to spreading kindness, one caring, thoughtful act at a time.

Whether the seeds for such acts of maitri, kindness, were already in him waiting to be discovered or he planted them as a way of dealing with his illness, Chris changed his world and the world around him through deep examination of his life and himself.

One of the goals of yoga, my teachers explained, is to answer a question: who are you? The question has a lot of what seem like obvious answers—I'm a woman, I'm a writer, I'm a wife, I'm a daughter, an aunt, a sister, a teacher . . . But to anyone who answered this way, Swami Satchidananda would say, were you always a writer? No. Always a spouse, a parent, your job occupation? No.

The point is not to have you questioning your entire reality, but to look within and find the truth—that you are a divine light, an eternal spirit. This truth will give you the strength and resilience to survive loss and will magnify your natural tendency toward love. Svadhyaya, self-study, is the tool that shines a light on treasures that have been within you since your beginning, and that, like diamonds forming from pressure, are beginning to take beautiful shape.

yoga mind practice:
Svadhyaya Meditation and List

Today, you'll get to know a beautiful new friend: yourself.

"Who are you?" is a question that can clear the path toward becoming the person you want to be. Svadhyaya, self-study, is an ongoing, lifelong process of discovery. Nothing is set in stone; today, simply set where you are now in your Yoga Mind journal.

Begin with your daily Deergha Swasam practice, sitting or lying down comfortably. By now, your body is becoming used to this new habit and is likely able to settle into a relaxed state faster. After a few rounds of three-part breathing practice, allow your breathing to find its own natural and comfortable rhythm for a few moments of pranayama meditation. Focus on the soothing rhythm of your inhalations and your exhalations.

Then begin repeating this mantra to yourself silently:

I am.

Repeat it to yourself in rhythm with your breath: inhale *I*, exhale *am*.

After a few minutes, release the meditation. In your Yoga Mind journal, write what you've discovered about yourself as you've gone along with this program. Be generous, writing down things you admire about yourself, that you've found funny or curious or surprising. If there's an attribute that reminds you of someone in your family, such as "I get my strength from Mom and Nana," write that down as an homage to them. Be loving and lavish in your praise to your true self.

And be as creative as you want while making out your svad-hyaya list. Use a calligraphy pen, colored markers, even crayons to make it little-kid joyful!

If you like, make a copy of this list and put it where you can see it every day.

steadiness and easefulness

Peaceful mind, easeful body, useful life.
—Sri Swami Satchidananda

Yoga poses, my teachers told me, are a mixture of sthiram and sookham, or steadiness and easefulness. You need strength and stability to hold the poses, and a sense of ease to do this without strain. The work you've done so far gives you that combination of steadiness and ease.

You've come to a point in this program where you're familiar with the tools and the way they work with you, sometimes through you. While you've definitely shaken things up, you know that you have within you what you need to regain balance and find your breath and your true center. And so, with this new grace, we keep going.

Last week you did a spiritual spring cleaning, identifying and releasing things you don't need—ideas about yourself and what you can or can't do, limiting beliefs, obstacles holding you back. By releasing them you've created space in your mind and heart. Now you can receive.

This next group of yoga tools will help you cultivate qualities you aspire to embody and find attributes you admire already within you.

✳ **Ishvara Pranidhana**—Known as "surrender of the self" in yoga, this tool helps us see the difference between loss and conscious, intentional release.

✳ **Karma**—Generally misunderstood as reward and punishment, this tool shows you how you can make a difference in the world, even through one simple act.

✳ **Karuna**—You'll never feel helpless again after learning about this tool that marries compassion with action.

✳ **Bhakti**—With the yoga of devotion, you'll be able to find the love in everything you do, turning even work you don't enjoy into an honorable spiritual endeavor.

✳ **Mudita**—Feeling happiness for others when they get something you want isn't easy. This tool makes it possible.

✳ **Svadharma**—Your unique calling, and how to find and express it without turning your back on the parts of your life that you love.

✻ **Sraddha**—In forming this strong sense of faith, "I don't know" is one of the most honest and powerful prayers we can say.

At this point in the program you know that every breath, inhaled and exhaled mindfully, is a prayer. And so, with a breath full of inspiration, we begin again, anew and renewing.

day 24

ishvara pranidhana

(ish-VAR-ah PRAN-ID-ha-na)
Surrender of the ego,
in order to be guided by truth.

When I let go of what I am, I become what I might be.
—Lao Tzu

The idea of surrendering the self can be scary. Why would anyone want to give up their identity, their idea of who they are? In fact, the word *surrender* alone puts people off; in our culture, surrender means losing.

This is a good time to remember the old saying about how sometimes we need to lose a battle in order to win a war.

Ishvara pranidhana is a continuation of the work you did yesterday with svadhyaya. As you remember, svadhyaya is the study of yourself. I'm hoping that you found a lot of diamonds in that exercise, but you may also have found a few lumps of coal you're not particularly thrilled about. This is where today's yoga tool comes in.

Ishvara pranidhana is surrendering ideas about yourself that keep you from growing and becoming your best, *truest* self. These ideas may be rooted in childhood, along with notions you've picked up along the way from relationships or experiences that didn't go the way you wanted them to. And their negative effects can be released. Ishvara pranidhana is the process by which you can surrender things that get in the way of who you really are—not someone else's idea of who you are or should be, not who you are as defined by a job or a set of circumstances, but your authentic, true self. This yoga tool of surrender allows you to be free of whatever would get in the way of being guided by the heart.

Just as I have discovered things I like about myself during difficult times, I've also found things that didn't serve me or anyone else well. When Marnie was sick, I prayed constantly, begging God to get her well again. I didn't belong to a specific religion but had, since childhood, always believed in Something. I didn't stop to think that in this case I might be confusing God with Santa Claus, and I begged, bargained, promised. And then Marnie died, despite all my praying.

Anger is a normal stage of grief, but I took it a step further and turned my back on God.

This was the loneliest time in my life. I felt empty, pointless, and useless, and I became apathetic about everything. I was now mourning two losses: one of my closest friends and my faith.

Losing Marnie was one of the worst things that ever happened to me. Losing my faith was one of the best things that ever happened to me.

The concept of faith that I'd had before, believing in something that would save my friend if I just prayed hard enough or did the right things, was flawed and formed out of desperation. I'm not trying to discourage people from praying; I pray all the time. I'm able to do that now with a heart full of faith because of ishvara pranidhana, which helped me see and surrender ideas that weren't helpful to me or anyone else.

The first one was not believing. Once I realized that not believing in anything didn't sit right in my bones, I knew I needed to find something to believe in again, and not my previous notion of a conditional, negotiating higher power. By meditating on ishvara pranidhana, I cleaned house, releasing everything I'd thought about God, spirit, the universe, even having a name for a higher power.

I'd forgiven myself for my desperate bargaining, but would whatever was listening forgive me? I'd barely begun my first tentative, shy prayer when I had the strong feeling that something had just communicated, in a warm and reassuring way, that there was nothing to forgive. It was pure, unconditional love.

That, I could believe in.

Being able to feel this was only possible after releasing what I thought I believed before. Later, I used ishvara pranidhana to get rid of useless ideas about myself: fear-based, self-sabotaging thoughts that I was not material for a loving, healthy relationship, that I wasn't strong, that I couldn't show up for my own life. Ishvara pranidhana helped me cleanse myself of these flawed and limiting ideas and open myself up to greater concepts of love.

When something terrible occurs—a tsunami, a school shooting in which innocent children are brutally murdered—anguish makes us ask what kind of God would allow this to happen. My feeling is that God is not the cause of natural disasters, not the force behind acts committed by individuals, or wars, or other events we can't make sense of. My belief is that God is what helps us *through* these things and is the love that drives us to help others. This is not meant to debate religious beliefs; this is my personal belief, one that has kept me free from despair and expanded my capacity for love and compassion.

This belief wasn't formed in the space of one prayer. It came over a long time of surrendering what I thought I knew about myself, a higher power, pretty much anything. This work was sometimes difficult and confusing but was consistently justified by the benefits. My new, indescribable faith in I-didn't-know-what increased my capacity for love. It gave me purpose. It showed me that I could be of service in a variety of situations. By surrendering what I thought I knew, I learned more and more.

During that time, ishvara pranidhana also brought the freeing magic of surrender to my on-again, off-again relationship. It helped me see that by hanging on to each other, my boyfriend and I were holding each other back. I was shown the difference between giving up and consciously, compassionately letting go. By looking at ending our relationship as a healthy step in honoring each other, we were able to part peaceably, respectfully, and with spiritual love.

The beautiful paradox of surrender is how much you gain. Nine months later, I went on a yoga retreat to Costa Rica. Also attending the retreat was a man who didn't fit any of my old ideas about "my type." That beautiful soul with the generous spirit became my husband. As I write this, Nathan and I have been together for twelve years. Each day, we surrender our old ideas and expectations, and each day, we fall in love a little more, and a little differently than we thought.

All of this became possible because I let go of the beliefs that were not part of my true self. I'm grateful to have lost the battle so that I could win the war through self-surrender.

yoga mind practice:
Surrender with Ishvara Pranidhana

The practice of ishvara pranidhana is tremendously freeing. It helps you release unhealthy habitual responses and stories about yourself. Sometimes you know what those are on a conscious level, but you don't have to be aware of specifics for ishvara pranidhana to work. You can trust in the divinely given gift of your intuition to weed out unhealthy thoughts and reactions and create fertile ground for truth.

In this meditation, you don't have to dwell on any attributes you've found that you don't like. Instead, you'll be focusing on the magic of ishvara pranidhana with a simple surrender mantra.

Begin with your regular Deergha Swasam yoga breathing practice. After a few rounds, allow your breathing to follow its own natural rhythm. Then silently repeat this mantra:

The more I release, the more I receive.

The mantra can sync with your breathing this way:

As you exhale: *The more I release . . .*

As you inhale: *. . . the more I receive.*

Continue for a few minutes. Release the mantra. After the meditation, note any feelings or experiences in your Yoga Mind journal. Trust that this simple exercise will begin working for you by placing the idea of release in your consciousness.

karma

(KAR-mah)

Every action has an effect.

Karma is generally understood as cause and effect, and generally misunderstood as good actions leading to good fortune and negative actions resulting in some form of punishment. That's a great device for novels and movies, but as we all know, things don't always work out that way in real life. Bad things do happen to good people, and there are plenty of people who've done terrible things and have yet to suffer even an annoying case of dandruff. So what is karma, really?

Yoga philosophy gives a deep explanation of karma and its many different forms. To simplify, some karmas, or actions, occurred in past lives, and the results are playing out in this one. It's said that we can only do our best to work them off in this lifetime. This may have been the ancient yogis' way of reconciling what we're still trying to understand today: why bad things happen to good people.

Even though Francesco hadn't known Marnie very well, her death affected him deeply. Her terminal illness had given him a sad perspective: where his situation could only improve, hers would only get worse. Being quadriplegic suddenly went from being a worst-case scenario to the lesser of two evils.

This didn't give him comfort of any kind. It seemed to bring up the same type of life questions he'd had when his injury was new, now more than a year ago, questions that could only be responded to with opinions and beliefs.

"I just don't understand it," he said, shaking his head (which was, in itself, a miracle). "Why did this happen? I mean, I understand the medical part, I know how Marnie died. But why?" he asked. "Why did she get sick? Why did I get injured? Why do these things have to happen?"

Francesco and I didn't usually have discussions like this. When we met each week, we were action-oriented, briefly catching up on each other's lives and then getting right down to the business of pranayama and meditation. We focused on improvement and moving forward. Sometimes, though, we had to pull over and mull over. That was today, this sunny fall afternoon. Down the road from Fran's house, tennis players ran from one side of the courts to the other, chasing the ball before it got too cold to play anymore, chasing these last warm days.

"There's a whole thing about actions in past lives in yoga," I said with a wave of my hand, not wanting to burden Fran with philosophical theories he might find troubling. I'd certainly had trouble with them. When a well-meaning yoga friend had attempted to process Fran's accident by talking about karma from another lifetime, I'd responded with a non-Sanskrit word: *bullshit*. "I don't really believe it," I told Francesco, so that I didn't curse in front of Nonni.

"So what *do* you think?" Fran asked, shifting slightly in his wheelchair—another miracle. "I've had people tell me that everything happens for a reason. People have said that my accident was God's will. I just can't—" He looked upset. "I don't want to believe that."

"I *don't* believe it," I said. "You really want to know what I think explains what happened to you, and what happened to Marnie? You want to hear my big cosmic theory, my take on the law of the universe that helps all of this make sense?"

"Yes," he said. "Yes, I want to know."

I leaned forward to make sure he'd catch every word. "Shit happens."

Fran's face went blank for a minute before breaking into a smile, and then he got the giggles. It's what I'd intended, but I also meant it. "That is the closest I can get to an explanation of why bad things happen to good people," I said. "Shit happens. You dive into a pool and end up in a wheelchair: File under 'shit happens.' Marnie—" I hesitated; it was still hard for me to say. "Marnie gets a form of cancer so far out of the demographic for the disease her doctors were ready to write medical papers about her . . ."

"Shit happens," Fran said, finishing for me. Now more somber, he nodded. "Of all the religious, philosophical, and spiritual theories I've heard, and I've heard a lot, I think I can work with this one."

"Don't hold me to it," I warned. "For all I know everything really is about what we did in past lives. But I believe what really matters is what we do in this life, now. I believe that every one of us is important and that we each have a contribution to make. A path, and a purpose."

As Fran took this in for a long moment, it was easy to read his thoughts. A purpose. He'd been dependent on other people since his accident over a year ago, and he would continue to be dependent on others for the foreseeable future. What was his purpose? Forget what past life or action from last summer had gotten him here. The far more interesting question was where he might go now.

Entertaining the possibility of a purpose alone began to light his path.

yoga mind practice:
The Easy Good Karma of Kindness

There is one simple act you can perform that can change another person's world, and your own: smile.

It sounds simplistic, maybe even hokey. But I can tell you that the times I've really believed that angels walk among us are the several occasions when I have been on the verge of tears in the street and some random stranger has smiled at me. The smiles are pure goodness, not compromised with requests, pity, attraction, or anything other than genuine human connection. People I don't know, passersby among hundreds in the streets of New York, will, on my worst days, smile at me. I've heard this from others as well. They'll be all down and blue, and someone will smile at them. The effect is transformative; they're lifted.

Other times, they're the angel, possessed of a sudden inexplicable desire to smile at someone they might not have even noticed before something made them look up from their phone to beam light at a stranger. They don't know why they did it. They only know that it gave them a glow, and it seemed to light up the other person's day a little, too.

I know the power of a smile. Maybe you do, too, if you've been on the receiving end of one of these small but powerful miracles.

Your Yoga Mind practice today is twofold. First, know this very important truth:

You matter.

You are important in the great and small schemes of things. You may not think so, but each of us creates the human equivalent of the Butterfly Effect, where the soft flap of a butterfly's wings in one part of the world can result in a great wind in another. You matter, and your actions have results. That is karma: action and result. It doesn't matter how quiet or benign your life may seem, or if you're in a wheelchair or a hospital bed. You have an effect on this world.

That brings us to the second part of your practice today: a smile. Just one is fine, or more if you feel so moved. You don't have to give a huge hundred-watt grin that might make people think you're crazy. (I'm thinking of New Yorkers, who are probably a tad warier than friendlier folks in other areas.) Just a smile, maybe a "Thank you" when you'd normally just plunk down money for your coffee, a "Have a good day" when you'd normally spend the whole elevator ride looking at your phone.

The tricky part is not expecting a result. There will be one, but you may not see it, and getting a result is not the point of this practice. During yoga teacher training at Integral Yoga, trainees are asked to perform an act of karma yoga, taking an action without expectation of a result other than the good feeling of having done the work. Karma yoga is usually something simple, like refilling the oil lamps or straightening up the kitchen cupboard. It's not about anyone being super-grateful or noticing that the shelves are now organized. It's about doing each task well for its own sake, without expectation of something in return.

So when you smile at someone today, release the expectation of thanks or a smile back. This is about your putting forth kindness—a small act that can change someone's day. They may be too surprised by your smile and the sudden connection to smile back.

Then again, you may have an experience that returns far more than you give.

generating peace

Don't hide your light under a bushel.
—The Bible

If you ever feel helpless to change circumstances beyond your control, or you feel that your actions have no effect on anyone but you, there is a profound job you can do: generating peace.

This isn't an easy world to live in, and it becomes more complicated with each passing year. There has been a lot of change, and more will come; about the only thing you can count on is uncertainty. That's no reason to hide in fear. In fact, it's all the more reason for each of us to step up to our work, which is generating peace.

What does that mean? Creating kindness everywhere you can, any time you can. You can go big if you want to, checking the organ donor box on your driver's license or volunteering your time to an organization. But even the smallest act of kindness can mean the world to someone. A thank-you, a dollar bill, a home for an animal in a shelter, a handwritten card instead of an email, a phone call instead of a text, a cup of coffee, a few words of encouragement, a hug. These are the small but profound moments that can put solid ground under someone's feet again.

As my teacher Rashmi says, "Be a light." Your actions can brighten the world, so shine your own light brightly by generating peace whenever and wherever you can.

day 26

~karuna~

(ka-ROO-na)
Compassion.

If you want others to be happy, practice compassion.
If you want to be happy, practice compassion.

—The Dalai Lama

I don't know the Sanskrit word for *pity*. We've never been introduced. When it comes to words that describe being moved to sorrow by another's misfortune, in yoga I heard a lot about karuna, or compassion. But there is more to it: karuna is empathetic sorrow united with action.

It may only be my emotional semantics, but *pity* has always seemed like it stands on the curb looking down at someone in the gutter and saying, "What a shame." The sadness may be sincere, but there's still that sense of other-ness, of separation. It's not a mean streak; it's natural for people to want to distance themselves from misfortune. There's so much misfortune in the world that it can become overwhelming, and we have to step back or we can barely face the day.

While pity stands on the curb bemoaning the ills of the world, karuna bends down to give a helping hand, a buck, a Kind bar. Karuna is moved to tears and moved to take action. Maybe only for one person, one animal, one abandoned lot that can become a community vegetable garden, but karuna knows that one can make a difference. Where pity thinks of other-ness, karuna thinks of others. This impassioned compassion isn't hard to find: it's in all of us. We just don't know it until someone gives us a chance to meet it.

Francesco's health coverage for physical therapy had long since dried up, and he didn't feel that the PT he'd been getting was going to make any real difference in his strength or mobility. He'd participated in a study in Detroit using a special bicycle that helped people with spinal cord injuries work their legs with an arm crank. The bike was part of Fran's vision to convert the Clarks' garage into a home gym, but that was going to cost a lot of money.

Up until this point, he'd resisted any suggestions about having a fund-raiser. "I don't want people feeling sorry for me," he told me one day, after describing the home gym and the expense.

"Okay, so don't call it a fund-raiser," I said. "Just throw a party."

He frowned. "A pity party?"

"I see your smart-aleck muscles are getting stronger," I said with a smirk, "but no, I meant a *party* party. A cool one. C'mon, it'd be fun."

"Maybe." Fran thought for a minute. "I don't like asking for help. I already need help for everything. I hate feeling this needy, this dependent."

I brought my chair closer to his wheelchair. "Fran, why do you think I come here every week?"

"Because we meditate. We do breathing exercises. Because you want to help me."

"Yeah, that's what I thought, too," I said. "That I was helping you. But don't you see the truth? You're the one who's been helping me."

He frowned. "How? You come all the way out here on the train every week, you taught me how to breathe . . ."

"And you're the one who let me. You're the one who said yes when I had the crazy idea about doing yoga breathing exercises in the hospital. You're the one who said you'd try meditation. You make time for me every week to come see you. Do you know what that's done for me?" I asked. "Do you know what it is to feel needed, to feel useful? That there's something I can do that can help someone? And you know what these past months have been like for me since Marnie died. That was devastating. But you were ready to meditate and breathe and gossip with me, and make me laugh and show me how you could move your arms a little more." I held his hand. "You gave my life meaning when you said yes. By letting me help you, you've helped me more than you can ever know."

We sat in the stillness for a long moment, the afternoon sunlight turning his room all hues of peach and rose. We were both a little teary. Then Fran sighed and said, "Jeez, all right already, I'll do it." He smiled. "Let's have a party."

The Francesco's Friends fund-raising event was Fran's first step into a new life. Not a new life in a wheelchair, but a new world filled with people who wanted to meet him, to know him, to befriend him, to help him. His former magazine colleagues had called in favors and arranged for a fancy space, donations of gourmet nibbles and an open bar, even swag bags filled with beauty products. The place was packed shoulder to shoulder with friends from Fran's childhood all the way through his career, family, neighbors, and strangers who'd heard about him and wanted to do what they could, even for someone they didn't know.

With his brother, Michael, pushing his wheelchair, Fran made a grand entrance, all dressed up in designer slacks and a shirt and tie. All eyes turned toward him. Where people used to stop and stare and give him looks of pity, now a big cheer went up, with hundreds of people clapping.

His smile, that huge, beaming grin, lit up the room. It was like one candle lighting hundreds at the same time, all of us beaming back at him. That gigantic, genuine smile of joy was Francesco's gift to everyone. Each person in that room felt they had done something good. Their lives had taken on new meaning—a richness that maybe hadn't been there before. Each had been given the gift of discovering the true joy that comes with helping another.

What we gave Francesco that night was enough to buy the bike and start his home gym. What he gave us was priceless.

yoga mind practice:
Karuna: Compassion with Action

Culturally, we're trained to think of ourselves first. In fact, you're reading this book so you can learn more about yourself and make positive changes. That's all good. The big secret is that one of the best things you can do for yourself is to do something for someone else.

Karuna, or compassion with action, doesn't have to be a huge, time-consuming gesture. It doesn't have to cost much, if anything. Karuna and its full benefits—to you and the object of your compassionate action—can be achieved with small gestures. Remember the Butterfly Effect. One small action on your part has the power to change someone else's world.

Today, discover karuna. It won't be hard to find; it's already inside you, waiting for its chance to bloom. In giving your help, you will be the true beneficiary, and what you gain will be far greater than whatever you give.

If *you* need help of some kind, your karuna practice today is simple: say yes. Tell someone what you need and let them do it for you, get it for you, give it to you. You will be giving them a great gift, and you'll get what you need. Everybody wins.

A small note: karuna is about helping those who want to be helped, not forcing help on someone. My friend Reverend Sam

Rudra Swartz, who is also in a wheelchair, once had to tell someone so hell-bent on doing the good deed of holding a door open for him that he was actually blocking Rudra's path. Be mindful in your karuna kindness.

Begin with your regular morning Deergha Swasam practice, sitting or lying down comfortably, keeping your spine long, creating space for your breath. After a few rounds of breathing in three parts, allow your breathing to find its own natural rhythm, and allow your awareness to rest gently on your inhalations and exhalations. See if there's a pause between each inhalation and exhalation, or if there's a continuous flow from one to the next. (There is no right or wrong; it's just a way of keeping your attention on your breathing.)

As you ease into this pranayama meditation, you can begin to silently repeat this phrase, the translation of a benevolent wish sent out at the end of yoga classes:

May the entire universe be filled with peace and joy, love and light.

The thought of filling the world with light will incline your thoughts toward where you can shine your light today. Somewhere along the way, you may see someone in need of your help, or think of someone who might need a hand or a phone call. You can also check out a list of karuna suggestions on my website for small actions that can have wonderful results.

day 27

bhakti

(BAHK-tee)
Devotion.

*Whatever we do can easily be transformed
into worship by our attitude.*

—Swami Satchidananda

Most of the instructors in yoga teacher training were senior yoga teachers, but occasionally we would have a guest lecture from one of the swamis in residence at the ashram. After one such lecture on yoga philosophy one day, the swami asked if we had any questions.

"I have one that's not about what we were reading," a student said. "Why do you and the other swamis here wear orange robes?"

"Out of all the aspects of yoga that can confound people, that's an interesting question," the swami said with a laugh.

"But a good one. The color orange represents flames. When we take sannyas, our vows, we symbolically toss attachment to the material world into a fire, becoming renunciates—we renounce the things regular householders have, like owning property, getting married, having children. We become monks, and we dedicate our lives to service." The swami, like the others at the ashram, was an American guy who'd had a regular job, but when he was a young man, something happened: he fell in love. Not with a person or an idea or a way of life, but with a higher power. The swami, along with monks, nuns, rabbis, the Dalai Lama, and others who join religious orders, chose to devote his entire life to a spiritual path. He did this from a sense of love.

At times I'd thought of becoming a renunciate. I'd met several sannyasin at Integral Yoga and at Ananda Ashram, where we went on retreat. Many of them had been there for decades. They'd found their guru, the person who helped them remove the darkness in their lives and find their divine light, and a path of spiritual life that sang to them so deeply that the material world didn't have any hold on them anymore.

The sannyasin still did things we do, such as visiting their families and going to the supermarket, and all of them had jobs at the ashram (for which they received room and board but no pay; swamis don't do bank accounts). Among many lifestyle differences, one was subtle and took time to notice: the swamis had a great attitude toward their work, even the least interesting tasks. Whether they were teaching philosophy or cleaning the ashram kitchen, the swamis managed to turn everything they did into something that looked like they were getting a lot out of it.

The secret was what they were putting into it.

For all my time at the ashram teaching and learning, I still hadn't figured out how to find the joy in every task in the outside world. I wasn't the only one, considering how much time my coworkers spent complaining in an average day. Having worked at many companies both on staff and as a temporary consultant, I can say that I've met a handful of people who really loved their jobs and a handful who really hated them. The majority fell in the middle, and their feelings could be affected by conditions that had nothing to do with the job. One colleague traveled over three hours to work and back each way—almost seven hours a day. That would be rough no matter how much you loved a job.

Liking a job could also become a test during stressful times, such as deadlines or when launching a new project. At magazines, the fur really flew during shipping, the period of time before magazine pages went to the printer. Every single thing was checked and double-checked by multiple people. Mistakes, missing information or photos, fact-checking, and changed minds could keep pages on desks and people at the office late into the night. I knew a few people who worked such late nights during deadlines they just skipped going home and slept overnight at the office.

"This story's going to be a monster," an editor said to me of a multipage special section I was putting together. There were dozens of interviews, an equal amount of photos and artwork to be sourced, credits, sidebars. "And it's scheduled to ship last, so it'll run up against other stories that lag," she added. "Don't make any plans for that week."

"I'll be here," I said. "We'll get it done."

"If the top editor doesn't make too many changes at the last minute." She sighed as she looked at the schedule. "I hate big stories with too many moving parts. And I hate late nights on deadline." Then she leaned back in her chair, reached over her computer, and tapped a photo on her bulletin board. "But I love this."

I stood and leaned over her desk so that I could see what she was talking about. Her fingertip traced the image of an eight-year-old in a pink sweater, her pigtails sticking out from both sides of her sweet, laughing face. "My daughter likes the school she goes to, and we like the house and neighborhood we live in," the editor said. "If that means I have to put in a couple of late nights here and there, I'll do it."

On the surface, this editor and the swami at the ashram seemed to have entirely different lives. What they had in common was greater than the sum of all the differences: bhakti, or devotion. The editor was married and had a child; owned a home and, presumably, all the stuff in it, from couch to clothing; had a job; received a paycheck; paid taxes. She was part of the material world. The swami had renounced everything. Like a monk, he wasn't married, had no kids, and technically didn't own anything; his robes were given to him, and he worked in exchange for housing and food at the ashram. Yet both were motivated to work, and do all the things that enabled them to do their work, by devotion.

By love.

Find the devotional love in whatever you do, and whatever you do will become easier. This is especially important for people who don't love their jobs. One of my students works at an insurance agency. He wouldn't exactly say he's in love with auto insurance, but he does love his wife and son. For decades, he has worked hard, for them. My friend Linda, a Reiki master, has given up many things so she can care for a retired racehorse who was headed for a scary finish line before Linda rescued her. Linda doesn't mind forgoing lattes out of love for Brandy. These people, who live in the material world, are as much bhakti yogis as the swami living the life of a renunciate at the ashram.

Every aspect of a swami's daily life is a devotion to God. The secret to their great attitude toward work, whether it's teaching yoga philosophy or doing the dishes after the evening meal, is that they consider everything they do to be an act of love. They don't think they're great because they have this attitude. They just think it's great that they get to do things that help create more peace in the world.

This is their bhakti, their devotion. It can be ours, too.

yoga mind practice:
Making Peace with Work Through Bhakti

Today's practice can transform the way you feel about your job, whatever your job is, wherever you work.

Begin with a few rounds of Deergha Swasam yoga breathing practice, and then do a few minutes of pranayama meditation, using your own breathing as your focus.

Then, in your Yoga Mind journal, make a list of who and what you love. Family is usually at the top of the list, and you can add your dogs, cats, or other animal friends. Extend the list to things you're glad to have: food in the kitchen, your home, the clothes that keep you warm and dry, the car that takes you to work (even if it's an old beater, if it gets you where you need to go, you probably have some appreciation for it). Now think of the things we can take for granted. Electricity. Heat. Clean water. The miracle of indoor plumbing! At times I catch myself marveling at the fact that I can take a hot shower. My grandparents did not grow up with that luxury.

By now you probably have a good list of things that fill you with love. Across from that list, write the thing that helps to support all the items in the left column: whatever you do for work.

Before we go further, it's worth looking at the Buddha's concept of Right Livelihood. This is the goal of finding a way to earn a living that doesn't bring harm to others. It's true that there are those who have jobs that do bring harm to others (such as working in slaughterhouses) in order to support their families. Were the Buddha around today, he might see them in an entirely different category than, say, people who make money by swindling the elderly with false promises of nonexistent real estate. In cases where someone causes more harm than they bring benefit, this bhakti list won't do as much good as finding a different line of work.

A job does more than bring financial support to your life. It gives you a sense of responsibility and an opportunity to make a contribution to the well-being of others. Think of interactions with the strangers we come into contact with every day, in person or over the phone. The man at the fish counter at my local supermarket is so friendly, everyone comes away from that counter smiling. Being a supermarket fishmonger isn't the easiest job in the world, but this guy does it so cheerfully, everyone who comes into contact with him feels uplifted. He's found the bhakti, the devotion, in his job.

Today, find your devotion. As you go through your day, think of the people and beings you love on your list. Think of how your actions contribute, directly and indirectly, to their well-being. If everything you do is for them in some way—including taking care of yourself so you can be of greater service to them—then everything you do will be an act of devotion.

mudita

(moo-DEE-tah)

Selfless joy for others.

If I am only happy for myself, many fewer chances for happiness. If I am happy when good things happen to other people, billions more chances to be happy.

—The Dalai Lama

Mudita is one of those "simple, not easy" concepts. Its definition is being happy for other people's accomplishments and the good news in their lives. Well, of course; only those miserly in spirit wouldn't be happy for another person who got something that brought them great joy, right? A deeper explanation of mudita, as the opposite of envy, brought the truth of the matter home: my first reaction on hearing other people's excited "Guess what?" was sometimes tinted green with jealousy.

Spring was coming, bringing with it new life in trees and all around, and slowly I was starting to emerge from mourning. The season of renewal invited taking stock, and what I found wasn't encouraging. My current consulting job was coming to an end, and once again I was in the position of wondering where my next paycheck would come from. I was alone, which I knew was better than the endless samskara of making up and breaking up with my ex, but the loneliness still hurt. I was at an age where I had to face the fact that getting married and having children wasn't going to just happen, as I'd somehow thought it would. One of the people I would've been able to talk about this with, and who would've cracked a joke that made me feel better instantly, was gone. I felt the empty space of Marnie every day. Having been at her bedside when she died, I never had the dim luxury of forgetting for a moment and picking up the phone to call her. I knew all the time that she was gone, and I felt her absence everywhere.

Right around this time a friend called with that breathless phrase that precedes an announcement: *Guess what?* Her novel was being published. She and I had written novels side by side, keeping each other going, a pair of writing running buddies. Now her book was going to be published and read by a ton of people. Mine was being used as a napping spot for my cat.

But the forces of good in the universe work in wonderful ways: I missed my friend's phone call, and her news went to my voice mail, so she wasn't subjected to my first reaction, which was some very unspiritual, non-yoga-teacher-like envy.

I was ashamed of myself. This person was a wonderful friend. What was wrong with me? Nothing, I realized; I'm human. I could practice yoga for years, learn about the tools and teach them, meditate, chant at the ashram all day, and light enough incense to make the world smell like patchouli, and that wouldn't change the fact that I'm a human being walking around with a heart full of human feelings. Yes, I felt a little envious. Acknowledging that helped keep it at a low level.

At the time, I was on a long walk to work, and I turned the walk into a meditation. I thought about mudita, the feeling of unselfish joy for others' good fortune, and Francesco's example of it. He'd shown me what mudita meant from my very first visit with him in the hospital. After assuring me that he was fine, what was the first thing he'd said to me? *How are* you *doing? Wait, didn't I hear you just graduated from a yoga teacher training course?* He'd been excited for me and wanted to hear more.

I don't know how truly interested Francesco was in my earning a yoga teacher training certificate, but by turning his attention to me and to all of his visitors, asking about their lives and being happy about their accomplishments, Francesco did actually feel joy for them. And he gave great joy to the people sharing their news with him.

As with everything he did, he went big. Francesco never stopped at merely being happy for someone; he would become their biggest cheerleader. The slightest hint of an idea was transformed by Fran's standards into an atom-splitting level of achievement. One day I mentioned a thought I had that might be something to write about someday, maybe. His reaction: "*Oh* my *God* you're writing a book! That is incredible! Tell me more!" His level of excitement could convince you that anything was possible.

He needed to believe that anything was possible, too.

Seeing this shining example of mudita brought me back to balance. Momentary clouds of envy passed. I was truly happy for my soon-to-be-published friend. She could tell from my shriek of joy when I called her.

Mudita is being as happy for someone else as we would be if their good news had happened to us. Mudita may not kick in automatically, but with some effort it becomes true, and the joy is compounded all around.

yoga mind practice:
Inspiration with Mudita Meditation

Envy is not only normal, it's natural, a part of our DNA. Our cavemen ancestors wanted the food or shelter other cavemen had because it was vital to their survival. Today, our modern versions of those prizes are promotions with nice raises, babies on the way, and other things we'd like to have—and sometimes have to watch others get before us. If your first reaction to some-one's good news is seeing a little green, that doesn't make you a bad person. Understanding that it just means you're human keeps the feeling from being exacerbated by shame.

Feeling unselfish joy for others is a muscle that needs to be worked to become stronger. It also requires a bit of what I call emotional yoga—making a feeling do a handstand so we can see its opposite. Turn envy upside down and it becomes inspi-ration. Instead of feeling jealous about what the other person has, you can look for the admirable qualities and work they did to get what you want. Usually, a great deal of effort goes into "good luck." My friend with the novel had researched numerous agents, written query letters (often thought of as being even more difficult than writing entire books), and done all the legwork that leads up to the "lucky break" of getting published. Think of all the actors and musicians who become "overnight sensations"—after decades of rejection and playing to empty theaters or nightclubs.

When someone has what you want, be inspired by them. Know that you can do what they did, or something similar. The empowerment of inspiration will open the gates to mudita, a feeling of unselfish joy.

Have to fake it 'til you make it? That's okay. Life is a spiritual gym. We get stronger by showing up and working at it.

Your practice today is strengthening the mudita muscle. Begin your morning Deergha Swasam practice, breathing in three parts for a few rounds before gradually returning your breathing to its natural rhythm. Then think of someone who got something you would also like to have. Don't dwell on this thought; just recall it momentarily.

Now bring to mind something you got that made you happy. A promotion, recognition of some sort, money you came into unexpectedly. Think of how your joy was compounded by others' feeling happy for you. This shows us an emotional equation: happiness becomes greater when shared.

Turn the envy upside down to cultivate inspiration. Think about the person who got something you wanted. Did she work hard for it? Did she get it after waiting a long time, patiently (or even impatiently)? Even lottery winners have taken an action in buying a ticket, probably many over the years.

Seeing that, know that you have the power to get what you want, too. I'm not talking about the notion that if you meditate on a new car long enough you'll get it. I believe that if you want something and you meditate on it, you'll gain insight into the work you have to do to get it. Francesco wasn't regaining movement by wishing. Every waking second of his day was spent working tirelessly toward his goals. Those seconds and every drop of sweat added up. Today, Fran can feed himself, crawl across a floor in case of an emergency, and do many other things. For someone who was told he would never move anything below his shoulders again, these achievements are his Everest climbs.

A mantra can help strengthen mudita. You can use it in today's meditation, and when you're watching someone get something you'd like very much to have. The mudita mantra is simple and sweet:

I want for you every happiness I would want for myself.

That mantra will give you something more precious than a new car, a promotion, or any of the other shiny pretty things we want: a vast and endless generosity of spirit. Mudita can make you feel like you're the richest person you know.

svadharma

(sva-DAR-ma)
Your unique life path;
your purpose.

There is a voice that doesn't use words. Listen.

—Rumi

I found Francesco in the kitchen, his wheelchair parked near the metal freestanding stove that warmed away the damp chill of this early spring day. There was still snow in the yard outside, but young green shoots were already poking out of the ground and trees, eager to start their lives.

Fran was in an uncharacteristically quiet mood. Not exactly down, more like contemplative. I asked him how he was doing, and he gave the facial equivalent of a shrug. "You know what," he said, "I'm bored."

This mundane feeling seemed like a relic of a time before catastrophic injuries, surgeries, clinical trials, wheelchairs, and home health care aides, but this wasn't the boredom of nothing being on TV or not having plans on a Saturday night. This was restlessness, the rustlings of hunger that urge a person to make changes and go out on a limb, even when that limb is still green and forming.

Fran sighed before thinking aloud. "It's not that I don't have things to do—I have physical therapy every day. But that can't be all there is to my life. I want to work, pay my family back for all they've invested in me, earn my keep. I want to *do something*." He paused and lifted his arm, testing out muscles still relearning how to work. "I'm regaining some movement, but big stuff, like walking, could take years," he said. "My doctors told me to get used to being in a wheelchair. I asked them what I was supposed to do—sit here and stare out the window for the rest of my life?"

Imagining Fran saying this in his usual polite but pointed way made me snort-laugh a little, and that made him smile. "Yeah, they didn't really have an answer for that," he said. "But I think I do."

"Okay . . ." I hadn't wanted to ask too much, unsure if there would be more to this than a rare venting of frustration. But Fran's expression showed that a decision had been made. "What's the plan?" I asked.

"I'm going to start my own company," he said. "I'm launching a skin-care line."

Fran explained that his father had, over decades in his cardiology practice, seen many patients in treatment for cancer; chemotherapy left their skin extremely sensitive. Their usual soaps, creams, or moisturizers were suddenly too harsh. Dr.

Clark used his longtime study of medicinal herbs and botanicals to make very gentle skin-care formulations. So far, they'd only been made in small batches for the patients who needed them.

"I want to take them public," Fran said. "They'll work for everybody. I want to get these cleansers and moisturizers in stores so they can help more people and give me something worthwhile to do. I'm starting a skin-care company," he said again. More to himself, and the world, than to me.

"Wow," I said, bowled over by his conviction. "Uh . . . Do you know how to do that? Start a skin-care company?"

"No," Fran admitted. Then his gigantic smile was back. "But I'll figure it out."

Dharma means "the path." Dharma can be the path of the Buddha's teachings, it can be the path of yoga, and it's also thought of as the path of cosmic order—the grand scheme of things. It can be a river of teachings or a river of life flowing as it should for reasons we can sometimes see the sense of and other times may never comprehend.

Within the larger path of dharma is svadharma, your own unique path. Svadharma is a calling. Its song is a message formed by your talents and skills, as well as where you are in your life. With svadharma, adversity doesn't block what you can achieve; it can be one of the ingredients that bring your achievements to life.

Francesco's life plans had taken a massive swerve, but he was determined that they wouldn't come to a complete stop. There was no downplaying what had happened, and nothing about his situation or his life was simple. Yet something inside him was acting like a GPS; after the swerve and some time to get his bearings, that something was saying, *Redirecting.* Time for a new plan, yes, but one that would utilize Fran's unique assets: his father's skin-care formulations, his connections to beauty editors at magazines and blogs, and his tireless energy for talking to people. (Shyness wasn't among the hurdles Fran would have to overcome.)

Svadharma can take us by surprise. In the yoga trainings I've taken and taught, a fairly large percentage of students will say, "I'm not sure what made me sign up for yoga teacher training. I only knew I had to do this."

A surprising number of that group will never go on to teach yoga.

I thought when I heard the statements of the people who felt compelled to take yoga teacher training, statements that mirrored my own experience of something inside that said—no, insisted—*Do this*, that these people were destined to become teachers. I thought it must be their svadharma to teach yoga. Yet only a few of them would eventually find themselves in front of a classroom of students. Having no inside information on the big picture (meditation has made me calmer, not psychic), I have a few theories. One is that these students were not ready *yet*. Another is that yoga teacher training may have been a redirect to something else that they were meant to do. Or it was meant to teach them something about themselves; maybe it wasn't the teaching certificate but something else they were meant to get from the intense spiritual training. Maybe what they learned will teach them how to be a better version of themselves, which will affect them and everyone around them and have a ripple effect outward. Maybe what they learned will be put to use to help someone else someday.

I was a writer who one day felt compelled to take yoga teacher training. I loved yoga, but the thought of teaching never occurred to me until the day came that I could think of nothing else, and I signed up for a basic training course. And at no other school but the one that taught me the most accessible form of yoga I'd ever seen, one where people of wildly differing levels of physicality were taught they could do yoga—even if they couldn't move at all. I showed up at Integral Yoga asking about teacher training on a Friday afternoon; I was told that the training began on Monday. Three weeks after I finished the training, Francesco had his accident. It could all be coincidence.

It could all be svadharma.

During my training, I didn't discover that I had any special talent for teaching yoga that would serve as proof of a destiny fulfilled. What I did have was a friend in need of something that would get him through one of the most difficult and terrifying times of his life, and a set of tools to help him. To this day I can't say with absolute certainty that it's part of my dharma to teach people yoga, but I have no doubt in my mind that my svadharma was to bring yoga to one person in particular. My own big life redirect may not have been about me at all.

In that sense, I was definitely on the right path. And Francesco was now on his.

yoga mind practice:
Finding Your Svadharma

Svadharma, your unique life path, is like a wise guidance counselor: it takes into consideration not only your talents and desires, but where you are in life. Your circumstances can be part of your path, not obstacles. People who have risen up from adversity to help others in similar situations have unique insight into the needs of those they help. A great example is the war veterans who have been helped by yoga and then go on to teach yoga to help their fellow veterans.

A person's svadharma can become what they do for a living, and it can also mean following a path outside of what they do for work. We often make decisions about the course of our lives based on the information we have, which makes sense. Svadharma can open doors of possibilities. If there's something you love and yearn to do, svadharma—your own unique path, your own unique way of doing something—will help you find a way to fit it into your life. If you don't have a specific yearning but feel the rustlings of that hunger for *something*, svadharma will help you find out what it is.

Thousands of people all over the world have been greatly inspired by an exercise in *The Artist's Way*, in which author Julia Cameron suggests making a list of other lives—different occupations they want or wanted to follow. Today's Yoga Mind practice is based on that exercise, with a bit of life résumé added.

Begin with your morning Deergha Swasam yoga breathing practice. After a few rounds, allow your breathing to find its natural pace, and use that as your focus for meditation. You can also practice japa with any mantra you like. Meditate in whatever way feels comfortable for you for a few minutes.

Then write in your Yoga Mind journal a list of paths you'd like to follow or that you once wanted to follow until you found yourself on a different road. Artist? Engineer? Nurse? Write whatever applies, however many you want.

Next, write a list of your talents and skills. Talents are something you feel you have an innate affinity for; skills are learned and honed. For example, you might have a chef's natural talent for being able to discern the ingredients in a dish by taste instead of being told, but you had to learn how to use a computer program. Make a list of both your natural talents and your learned skills. If you want, take your Yoga Mind journal with you and write things as they come to you throughout the day.

Two things to know as you do this exercise: First, finding your svadharma doesn't mean suddenly quitting your job and walking away from your life. It means you'll be guided by your own intuition about the extent to which your svadharma becomes a part of your life.

Second, limitations are challenges, not dead ends. Jean-Dominique Bauby was living an enviable life when he had a stroke that left him completely paralyzed and mute, his movements limited to the ability to blink his left eye. Yet through painstaking work, he was able to communicate with his doctors and aides, and eventually to write an extraordinary, poetic

memoir of his life and experiences, *The Diving Bell and the But-*
terfly. The book was also made into a film. His circumstances,
as daunting as can be imagined, did not stop Jean-Dominique
from communicating with the people he loved and even creating
a work of lasting beauty that continues to inspire people. His
circumstances were woven into his svadharma.

By the end of this day you may begin to see patterns of your
svadharma emerging. You may see a connection between your IT
skills and your desire to mentor at-risk youth. You may wonder
how you missed the connection between your quilting talents
and a desire to teach and lead sewing circles at the local senior
center, or do a series of quilting videos for an online workshop.
Who knows what you can do?

It's time for you to find out, and to walk your own unique
life path.

sraddha

(shrah-DAH)

Faith.

If you have faith, you can see God in everything.

—Swami Satchidananda

Faith. Belief. This is sraddha. Faith in what? Belief in what? That's not the important part.

Once again, I was in a place of not knowing. Just as when I'd first seen Francesco in the hospital and been amazed—not in a good way—by the vastly empty feeling of not knowing what to do, I found myself in a state of uncertainty, this time about my own life. What now?

I had come not to a fork in the road but to a wide-open space with no discernible path. I'd begun to see my career as a series of chairs at various interchangeable desks, each job playing out the same way: I went into different offices that all looked the same; worked with good people; wrote about various things for varying periods of time, a month here, a few years there, knowing all the while that things would come to an end. I realized that for me there was no feeling of permanence because at heart I needed to walk my own path. The jobs were fine and I was grateful for them, but they were not the endgame, the hard-won "result," and climbing the corporate ladder meant nothing to me. That was all I could gather. Behind those questioning thoughts, waiting patiently, was a sense that I should be doing something else. But what?

I didn't know.

Losing myself in a relationship wasn't an option. My on-again, off-again boyfriend and I had finally achieved relationship success—which meant, for us, breaking up permanently. We'd agreed not to speak; too tempting to lapse back into shared jokes, finishing each other's sentences, talking about movies, and making plans to get together as friends. Our now months-long silence had the peaceable quality of finality. In that, I experienced freedom from a cycle of instant gratification and long-term suffering.

Francesco was busier than ever. In addition to launching his skin-care company, Clark's Botanicals, he'd been asked to join the Christopher and Dana Reeve Foundation as a national ambassador. His days were filled with designing logos and choosing packaging for the products, making appearances, doing media interviews, and physical therapy. When our weekly visits became every other week, and then monthly, I was both wistful and deeply gratified; this had been our goal all along. Francesco had wanted independence, and although that goal wasn't complete, he was on the way. He'd learned to meditate and do his pranayama on his own. He didn't need to need more help, he needed to find his own way to live his own life. He'd learned to do his yoga. And I learned that I couldn't define myself by him, either; it was time for me to do my yoga, travel my path, live my life.

In the Hindu pantheon, there is a goddess named Kali who helps spiritual travelers by systematically, sometimes violently, removing anything that their ego can hold on to. I thought about Kali Ma, the Fierce Mother, who takes sharp toys away from her children as I reflected on not being able to form a false sense of self through a job title, relationship status, or even the path of being a yoga teacher. I could lead classes in asana, but as far as being a teacher, I knew now that I'd been Francesco's student as he'd lived the teachings of yoga, showing me week after week what the tools truly meant.

So . . . now what?

Now that I stood, spiritually speaking, in this open field of possibilities, I saw that I'd been looking for answers. That not-knowing feeling had spooked me into feelings of attachment to unstable things and craving absolutes. But the cumulative effect of seeing yoga's tools in action through Francesco's living example of them, and putting them into practice myself, had turned uncertainty into a form of faith. Before, my faith was based on results, contingent upon everything turning out okay, by my definition. Now I understood faith as a verb, an ongoing action. Faith was like breathing; it wasn't something I got, it was something to be done. Inhale. Exhale. Believe. Have faith.

This was a new faith, one that came without instructions and didn't make any guarantees other than that it would be with me always. In truth, everything is not going to be okay; watching Marnie die taught me that. This faith, this type of belief, didn't say everything would be okay; it said *I* could be okay—maybe not when something soul-wrenching was happening, but eventually.

This faith is sraddha.

Sraddha is like a surfboard you've made yourself from experience and skill and doggedness, and with this faith you ride the waves of life. You may fall off from time to time, just as surfers fall off their boards. This is why they wear a leash, a tether that they wrap around one ankle to connect them to the surfboard. That way, a surfer never loses their board to a wipeout in a big wave. They're thin, these leashes, but they're strong. We all have these. We are all connected to our faith.

Just as svadharma is your own unique path, sraddha is your own personal faith. You can believe in a specific religion, yet your faith is still your own, because you're the one exercising it. The way it flows through you, and the way you act on it, is yours. You can have strong faith in a spiritual path of your own definition. Even those who say they don't believe in anything believe in that.

Francesco wanted more than anything to walk again. That hadn't happened, not yet, anyway, but he was undeniably moving forward. Faith, I saw, was not a matter of getting or even being but of doing. Of making the choice, again and again, as many times as was necessary, to climb back on the surfboard and believe. To sometimes not really know what you were believing in, and to believe anyway.

Sraddha was the form of faith that turned "I don't know" into a most honest prayer. I had no idea what I should do next, or where to go, or who I was or could be. Without faith, this could have thrown me into a crisis. With faith, I became free of plans affected by things outside myself and my own narrow, fear-based views. In saying, *I don't know*, I was saying to something far greater than myself, *You do*.

I exercised sraddha. I breathed it, I worked it. My faith was that I would be guided toward whatever step was next and whatever work I had to do. I had faith in something, the name of which I didn't know, but I felt its presence profoundly in my heart.

yoga mind practice:
Living Sraddha

This isn't an exercise that takes one day, or thirty. You've been doing this exercise since you were born—some would say since before you were born—and you'll be doing it for the rest of your days. Your practice is to find your own form of faith, your own sraddha.

This may change over time. It may have changed since you set that sankalpa on day one of this program. You may now know more about yourself, and less about your beliefs, than before. I hope that they've become as vast as the sky.

That doesn't mean changing your religion, or changing who you are. It means your sense of faith and love and your belief in yourself and in possibilities have gotten bigger. I find it wonderful to think that I only need faith the size of a mustard seed (and those things are *tiny*) to begin to understand that love is everywhere, and that its possibilities are endless.

If you say certain prayers, keep saying them. Sraddha will only enhance them and make them more meaningful to you. If you don't say prayers, maybe you want to try. If you meditate, your experiences may become deeper. If you don't meditate, you have your Deergha Swasam practice. Your every breath is a prayer, a declaration of love for life. And when someone stops breathing, as my friend did one night, sraddha tells us that they become part of that which breathes life into us. As Marnie had been all along. As you are now, and always will be.

Your faith can be the knowledge that the spirit—the divine light within you, the people you love, and all beings—is eternal. When you have that, you have everything you need.

Spiritually Surfing Life's Waves

"Okay, you can come in now."

This time, when I hear the same words I remember from sixteen years ago, it's not Francesco's sister leading me into his hospital room but a hostess leading me to a back section of a restaurant: a much better setting, and a far more joyous way to get together with Fran.

This time, we aren't meeting to meditate and practice pranayama together. We're just having dinner with some friends. This is what we were doing all that spiritual work for—to be able to go out into the world and work, be in relationships, learn who we can be and what we can do. And have some Chinese food on a Friday night.

My husband, Nathan, takes my hand and we follow the hostess to a big circular table, where we join Geri and her daughter, Nathalie, who was just a baby when Geri, Fran, and I worked together at *Mademoiselle*. Now Nathalie's seventeen, a beautiful young mademoiselle herself, underscoring how time passes. Yet the things that are important to us remain true and vibrant; I don't think a single day in these sixteen years has gone by that I haven't thought about Marnie and imagined what she'd say in a given situation, heard her guffawing laugh. She's always with me.

At the outside of the banquette, which becomes the head of the table, is Francesco. I don't see the person who felt there was no reason to change out of his hospital pants because it didn't matter. He's wearing Italian slacks and a cashmere sweater—his usual work uniform. As the CEO of his own company, he now always wants to look his best even if he's only working from home with his assistants and aides. More often than not, he's traveling into New York City to meet with beauty editors and do guest segments for Clark's Botanicals on QVC. Nathan often says that Fran does more from a wheelchair than most people without such hindrances do.

Francesco is living his yoga, using his tools. He didn't wait until he could walk to engage with life again. He's still in his wheelchair and needs help for his basic needs, though no longer to eat. It's not easy; he needs to be slow, methodical, get the food at the right angle. But that small act of independence, of being able to take a bite of what he wants when he wants, is delicious.

Things don't always turn out the way we want them to. When that happens, we do our best. We adjust. We adapt. We fall, and we get back up again. We ask for help and give it. In giving we receive, and in receiving, we give. Everything changes— jobs, relationships, homes, our bodies. Change can be upsetting, at times even devastating. And it can be joyful, I think as I look at Nathan. Without change, I would never have met him.

If we remember yoga's true lesson, that we can go with the flow of change, we learn the value of every experience in our lives.

Life is an ocean of time, and the events we go through are its waves. Some of these waves will be smooth and calm. Others will be rock 'n' roll, and still others will cause you to wipe out.

What you have learned over these thirty days will get you back on your surfboard. This program has come to an end, and yet the end is a new beginning—the beginning of satya, the truth: the tools are with you, always. Your own natural ability to work them is the surfboard on which you ride the waves of life. Sometimes that board may take different shapes, look different, feel different under your feet. At times you may fall off.

Don't be afraid. Just climb back on, spiritual surfer.

And take a deep breath.

yoga tools by category

This guide will help you find yoga tools for specific needs quickly.

Mantras/Affirmations
Asteya, non-stealing, page 129
Ishvara pranidhana, surrender, page 213
Japa, repetition of a mantra, page 167
Maitri, kindness, page 97
Mantra, mind protection, page 53
Mudita, selfless joy for others, page 241
Pratipaksha Bhavana, the Yoga Thought-Swap Trick, page 157
Santosha, contentment, page 141
Saucha, purity, page 113
Svadhyaya, self-knowledge, page 201

Self-Care

To Help Counteract Negative Thinking

To Use in Relationships with Others

To Improve Focus

For Strength in Challenging Times

Sutra 1.14, never give up, page 151

Tapas, learn from the burn, page 195

Titiksha, endurance, page 189

For Happiness

Bhakti, devotion, page 233

Karuna, compassion, page 227

Maitri, kindness, page 97

Mudita, selfless joy for others, page 241

Santosha, contentment, page 141

Yoga for Populations with Specific Needs

These are groups, organizations, and sources of information for people in specialized situations who can benefit from yoga. (Note: Some of these recommendations are based on my experience of having taken trainings with them; others are based on recommendations from other yoga instructors. I do not receive remuneration from them for listing them here.)

DianneBondyYoga.com, BigYogaOnline.com

Both Dianne Bondy (Dianne Bondy Yoga) and Meera Patricia Kerr (BigYogaOnline) are leading a revolution in making yoga accessible for plus-size students.

AbundantWellBeing.com

People working with cardiac and cancer issues will find classes, trainings, and more at Nischala Joy Devi's site.

Accessible Yoga, AccessibleYoga.org
This organization specializes in adapting yoga for those who do not have access to traditional classes for different physical abilities and for underserved communities.

Yoga for Arthritis, Arthritis.yoga
A resource for people living with arthritis, both rheumatoid and osteoarthritis, as well as teachers who want to be trained in this line of adaptable yoga.

Therapeutic Yoga, TherapeuticYoga.com
Anyone who wants to incorporate wellness into their treatment plan for illness will find Cheri Clampett's teachings beneficial.

Yoga for the Special Child, SpecialYoga.com
Yoga therapist and author Sonia Sumar has been teaching students and training yoga instructors in the beneficial adaptation of yoga for children with autism.

Yoga for Addiction
For those in recovery, yoga is a beneficial tool *in conjunction with* appropriate treatment, not as a substitute. Here are some resources that adapt yoga to work with recovery.

The Yoga of Recovery, YogaofRecovery.com
Durga Leela teaches both students and yoga instructors about yoga as a complementary practice for recovery.

Yoga of Recovery at Kripalu, Kripalu.org
Aruni Nan Futuronsky has been with Kripalu for twenty years

and specializes in yoga for people in recovery. Ask about special recovery-oriented programs.

Y12SR, Yoga of 12-Step Recovery, Y12SR.com
Nikki Myers incorporates the tools of twelve-step-based recovery programs into yoga classes for unique recovery meetings.

Recovery 2.0, Recovery2Point0.com
Tommy Rosen creates podcasts and programs for those seeking to use yoga as a basis for their recovery.

Caregivers

People who take care of children and adults with specialized needs also need to take care of themselves. For planned or emergency respite care, contact:

ARCH (Access to Respite Care and Help), the National Respite Network, RespiteLocator.org.
Leeza's Care Connection, Leeza Gibbons's network for caregivers, LeezasCareConnection.org.

Integral Yoga

For more information about Integral Yoga, Swami Satchidananda, classes, teacher trainings, and yoga in general, please visit IntegralYoga.org and iyiny.org.

kritajna: gratitude

A great many people help to make a book possible, and a great many people help a person to become all that they can be. I am filled with immeasurable gratitude for the following people who helped this book to be and helped me to be a channel of it. I strive to be worthy of their love and support.

Francesco Clark was already a good friend, but when one day he said yes to an improbable idea that came to me, he helped me achieve a sense of usefulness I'd never experienced before. Without him, this book would not exist, and I would not have found my purpose. My love to you, my dear friend. My gratitude also to the entire Clark family for their strength, courage, love, and spiritual generosity.

I bow in gratitude to the divine lights at Integral Yoga Institute. I give thanks beyond words to my teachers Kali Morse, Rashmi Galliano, Swami Asokananda, Swami Ramananda, Swami Chidananda, Swami Vidyananda, Chandra Jo Sgammato, Sam Rudra

Swartz, Jean Boudwin, Boris Bhagavan Pisman, and Rudra Sisco. I bow in gratitude to Prem Anjali, Mataji, Swami Vidyananda, and the rest of the staff and sannyasin of Yogaville Ashram in Virginia and Ananda Ashram in New York. I'm grateful to all the beautiful students who have given me the gift of allowing me to serve them as a teacher and teacher trainer. Most of all I give thanks to Sri Swami Satchidananda. His teachings and selflessness in a life dedicated to service and helping others illuminated our path, and we carry that light on in our service to others. *Jai Gurudev!*

My agent, Jill Marsal of Marsal Lyon Literary Agency, said something that every author wants to hear: "I want you to write this book because I need it." I kept what she said in mind like a mantra to take a raw idea and hone it into this book and program. Her patience is a true example of yoga.

Michele Martin, Diana Ventimiglia, Cindy Ratzlaff, and Karen Adelson—my publishing team—connected with this book on a deep level and saw how it could help people through all types of life events. Their vision exceeded what I thought was possible in sharing these teachings with the world. I am honored to be part of their commitment to creating positive change, and their creativity.

I give thanks to yoga teachers that I have experienced and who have helped shape my practice: Sharon Gannon and David Life of Jivamukti Yoga, Cindy Lee of OM Yoga, Brian Liem of OM and Now Yoga, Shiva Rea, Tao Porchon Lynch, Cheri Clampett and Arturo Peal, and many others. Special thanks to Jivana Heyman, founder of Accessible Yoga, Steffany Moonaz and Nancy O'Brien of Yoga for Arthritis, and everyone who has put their hearts and energy into ways to make yoga available to everyone. Gratitude to Stephen Cope, whose book *Yoga and the Quest for the True Self* opened my mind and heart to the possibilities of true yoga, and whose book *The Great Work of Your Life* inspired me to follow my svadharma.

Creative inspiration comes in many forms, and watching people express their creativity has helped me find my own path. My thanks to Danny Gregory, Koosje Koene, Morgan Green, and all the teachers and students at Sketchbook Skool for their art and ideas. Thanks to Jimmi Simpson for showing what following one's dharma can be like, and for the dandelion video. Thank you to Amy Gross, my incredibly serene editor in chief, Deborah Way, and all the editors I worked with at *O, The Oprah Magazine*. Big thanks to all my English teachers for showing me how to fall in love with the written word. I know it was challenging to teach classrooms full of rowdy kids, but the one in the back with the thick glasses really heard you.

I have a small and amazing sangha of friends who have performed the incredible service of listening, being there, and supporting me. I give immense gratitude to David Keeps, Hope Tarr, Stephanie Krikorian, Sherri Rifkin, Amanda Siegelson, Geri Richter Campbell and Nathalie Campbell, Alice Uniman, Linda Maglionico, and many others who know who they are. Special thanks to Gerri Brownstein for helping me breathe through rough patches. My love goes to Marnie's Angels—her husband, Pascal, her best friends, Anne-Marie and Rima, and her family.

My family sangha is extended and delightful, and I am so grateful for this large group, including my beautiful sisters, Amanda, Luisa, Rebecca, and Laurie, and their partners and children; Sheila Colón, Ruth Ashby-Colón, and Ernie Colón; Caleb Tweti; my godmother, Barbara Haspel-Habif; and my cousins and their kids. To my parents, David and Carolyn, I can't say thank you enough; I can only try to make you proud.

To the love of my life, Nathan. I went on a yoga retreat to Costa Rica because it was a safe vacation for a single woman going through a confusing time in her life. This trip allowed me to find yoga—union—with my true self, and then with the man who would become my husband. Words can only convey so much of how I feel about you, my love, but hopefully my actions speak for me.

✳

My greatest thanks go to you, dear reader and sangha member. You've taken brave steps on this path of self-discovery and contribution to the world, and we've taken those steps together. At the end of yoga teacher training, we tell the students who have completed the course that even though they now go forward and take what they've learned out into the world, they are always members of the sangha. You are a member of this sangha, and you always will be.

This is the end of the book and the beginning of your new path. We still travel this path together, unique and yet connected, our road lit by the divine light that shines within each of us and all of us.

May your divine light illuminate your path, may its radiance help others to shine, may you know that these tools of yoga are always with you and within you. This book was once your guide; may it now be a companion on your path. *Jai!*

about the author

Suzan Colón is a former senior editor of *O, The Oprah Magazine* and an Integral Yoga Institute yoga teacher and teacher trainer. Suzan's writing has appeared in four *Oprah Magazine* "best of" anthologies, *Details, Good Housekeeping, Harper's Bazaar, The Huffington Post,* and many other media outlets. Suzan has been a yoga practitioner for twenty-five years and has been trained in basic and intermediate levels of yoga, Therapeutic Yoga, and Yoga for Arthritis. She is the creator of the iTunes app Take a Yoga Break, which was named one of *Fast Company*'s Innovation Agents of 2014. Suzan lives in the New York area with her husband, Nathan. Visit her at SuzanColon.com.

by noon
on
B+G Sports   Saturday
2444 East Main Street
Watrbury
Donna Matt $ oo
(203) 757·2571
[→ Embroidery!

Noelle
Munstrane